Prayers Responsively

Responsive General Prayers for the Three-Year Lectionary

Theodore P. Bornhoeft

Publishing House
St. Louis

Biblical references in the prayers in this publication are from the Revised Standard Version of the Bible, copyrighted 1946, 1952 © 1971, 1973. Used by permission.

Copyright © 1984 Concordia Publishing House
3558 S. Jefferson Avenue
St. Louis, Missouri 63118
Printed in the United States of America

Permission is herewith granted to reproduce the prayers in this book for congregational use. Except for this usage, no part of this publication may be reproduced for sale or distribution, stored in a retrieval system, or transmitted, in any form or by any means, electronic, mechanical, photocopying, recording, or otherwise, without the prior written permission of Concordia Publishing House.

Library of Congress Cataloging in Publication Data

Bornhoeft, Theodore P.
    Prayers responsively.

  1. Prayers.   2. Responsive worship.   I. Title
BV245.B617 1984   264'.13   83-15112
ISBN 0-570-03922-3

2 3 4 5 6 7 8 9 10 **VP** 93 92 91 90 89 88

CONTENTS

Preface	4
Prayers for Sundays and Major Festivals: Series A	
Advent Season	7
Christmas Season	11
Epiphany Season	14
Lenten Season	24
Holy Week	30
Easter Season	33
The Season after Pentecost	42
Prayers for Sundays and Major Festivals: Series B	
Advent Season	74
Christmas Season	78
Epiphany Season	81
Lenten Season	91
Holy Week	97
Easter Season	100
The Season after Pentecost	109
Prayers for Sundays and Major Festivals: Series C	
Advent Season	140
Christmas Season	144
Epiphany Season	147
Lenten Season	157
Holy Week	163
Easter Season	166
The Season after Pentecost	175
Prayers for Minor Festivals and Occasions: Series A, B, C	
New Year's Day (The Circumcision of Our Lord)	206
Reformation Day	207
Day of National Thanksgiving	208

PREFACE

The responsive prayers in this book incorporate the concerns of the General Prayer of the Church with the appointed Scripture readings from the three-year lectionary. Prayers have been provided for each Sunday and commonly observed major and minor festival and occasion of the church year. Where an alternate gospel reading is indicated in the lectionary, an alternate prayer has been provided.

These prayers are written responsively to maintain the attention of the congregation and relieve the tedium of an unbroken form. The pastor's versicle is printed in roman (plain) type, while the congregational response is printed in boldface type. Opportunity for special intercession, either silent or spoken, is provided in each prayer. For ease of usage the three cycles of the three-year lectionary are listed separately. Congregations with access to photocopy equipment are invited to duplicate the prayers directly from this book.

Dr. Henry E. Jacobs states that the purpose of the General Prayer of the Church is "to present most forcefully the Church as the Communion of Saints, where the end of all our prayers for men is that they may be brought to repentance and faith and through repentance and faith experience the fullness of the divine blessing, both temporal and eternal."[1] To that end these prayers are offered.

---

[1] Henry E. Jacobs, *The Lutheran Movement in England During the Reigns of Henry VIII and Edward VI, and Its Literary Monuments* Rev. ed. (Philadelphia: Frederick, 1892), p. 303.

PRAYERS FOR SUNDAYS AND MAJOR FESTIVALS

Series A

FIRST SUNDAY IN ADVENT

By Your grace, O Lord, we enter a new church year. **We praise You for Your goodness, which has followed us through many generations.** Yours is the kingdom, the power, and the glory. **We thank You for giving to a world in darkness a ray of hope in the promise of the Messiah.** Graciously help us to rejoice in that promise and prepare for His coming.

As the citizens of Jerusalem welcomed Christ with shouts of hosanna, grant that we too rejoice in His coming. Unlike the citizens of Jerusalem, let us recognize Him as our Savior from sin and our hope for everlasting life.

We long for that peace promised by Isaiah: when nations "shall beat their swords into plowshares and their spears into pruning hooks...." **Help us to realize that Christ came to bring a higher and more enduring peace between us and Your divine majesty.** As a King whose kingdom is not of this world, but from everlasting to everlasting, **grant that Christ may always rule our hearts.**

Keep us awake and alert that we may always be found ready for the end time when He shall suddenly appear as the Judge of all. **Help us to conduct ourselves as becomes those who bear Your name—**"not in revelry and drunkeness, not in debauchery and licentiousness, not in quarreling and jealousy." **Bless our witness to His peace, which comes as Your gift to us.**

(*Here special intercessions, silent or spoken, may be made. If spoken, each portion concludes:* Lord, in Your mercy, **hear our prayer.**)

Grant, O Lord, that our lips and lives be a reflection of hearts that are truly thankful for Your great mercy. **This we ask in the name of the King of kings and the Lord of lords, our Savior, Jesus Christ. Amen**

SECOND SUNDAY IN ADVENT

Almighty God, whose ears are always open to our prayers, hear now the prayers of Your people. **We thank You for Your sure Word of Prophecy and its fulfillment in the Word made flesh, Jesus Christ, our Lord.**

Since by birth, many of us are not part of Your chosen people, Israel, we thank You that in Your sure Word of Prophecy You have included us Gentiles. **We glorify You, O Lord, for bringing forth a shoot from the stump of Jesse, the Branch, Jesus Christ, our Lord.** We thank You, O Lord, for anointing Him with Your Spirit, the Spirit of wisdom and of understanding, the Spirit of counsel and of might.

Stir up our hearts, O Lord, and fill us with all joy and peace in believing. May we abound in hope through the power of Your Holy Spirit. **Empower us to serve and love You with pure hearts and obey You with willing hands.** As You have welcomed us into Your fellowship in Christ, may we welcome many others. **Give us one voice to glorify You as the God and Father of our Lord Jesus Christ.**

Help us to demonstrate Christ as a sign of hope to the world. **Grant us the courage to call the world to repentance and point to Jesus Christ as the only hope for salvation.** Extend Your healing hand to the sick, and be a companion to the lonely.

(*Here special intercessions, silent or spoken, may be made. If spoken, each portion concludes:* Lord, in Your mercy, **hear our prayer.**)

Bless those entrusted with leading our nation, and grant peace to the world. **We pray in Jesus' name. Amen**

THIRD SUNDAY IN ADVENT

Lord God of Zion, who reigns from everlasting to everlasting, governing the lives of all generations, **we come before You in awe and reverence.** Accept our praise and adoration for Your providence, which has sustained us to this present hour. **Accept our grateful thanks for the abundant blessings You have bestowed on us through Jesus Christ.**

We confess that we are often blind to the greatness of Your love. **We have often been deaf to the hopefulness of Your promises.** We have often been speechless in extolling Your name. **We have lacked patience in dealing with one another.** We have eaten our fill and failed to show proper consideration for the hungry. **For these, our many transgressions, forgive us, O Lord.**

By the power of Your Holy Spirit strengthen our weak hands and make firm our feeble knees. **Give us fearless hearts, and open our eyes to the abundance of Your mercy.** Help us to meet the needs of humanity. **Keep us patient in the expectation of Your coming.** Raise us from the dead leprosy of our sin to the lively hope of salvation through Christ.

(*Here special intercessions, silent or spoken, may be made. If spoken, each portion concludes:* Lord, in Your mercy, **hear our prayer.**)

Prepare a highway in the wilderness of our hearts so that the Christ, whose birthday we shall soon celebrate, **may enter and dwell within us eternally. In His name we pray. Amen**

FOURTH SUNDAY IN ADVENT

O Lord of hosts and King of glory, we come before You eagerly anticipating the celebration of Your Son's birth. **We give You thanks for clearly identifying Him through Your prophet as the one to be born of a virgin.** We thank You that through Your Word we can clearly trace His earthly ancestry to King David. **We are sure that He who was born in Bethlehem is truly the one You promised to send: our Savior.** We are grateful that in predicting His coming You clearly indicated His purpose. **We are thankful You called Him Immanuel, reminding us that in Him You are always with us.**

Even though, O Lord, You have clearly identified our Savior in Your Word, our minds are unable to comprehend the mystery of the events that have taken place. **Send us Your Holy Spirit that we may believe those mysteries we cannot understand.** As we have found in Him the source of the peace that fills our hearts, **empower us with Your Holy Spirit to proclaim Him as the Savior of the world.**

As the day approaches when He shall come as the Judge of all nations, keep us mindful of the urgency of our task. **Grant us Your Holy Spirit that we may go quickly and spread the Good News of Your salvation.** May our witness result in the salvation of many souls before Your time of grace comes to a close and it is no longer possible for anyone to be saved.

(*Here special intercessions, silent or spoken, may be made. If spoken, each portion concludes:* Lord, in Your mercy, **hear our prayer.**)

May Your peace rule our hearts as we joyfully celebrate the birth of Your Son, our Savior, **in whose name we pray. Amen**

THE NATIVITY OF OUR LORD

Praise, honor, and glory to You, O Lord our God. **With angels and archangels we magnify Your name: "Glory to God in the highest, and on earth peace among men with whom He is pleased."** We adore Your divine goodness and praise You for sending deliverance to Zion and for including us in the fulfillment of Your promises.

Even though we have no merit or worthiness within us, You have once again this Christmas assured us of Your love. Instead of justly punishing us, You have sent us salvation in the birth of Your Son. **In spite of our many transgressions You have made salvation possible in this gift of mercy.**

For rejoicing more in earthbound gifts than in Your heaven-sent gift, forgive us, O Lord. **For telling others more about earthly treasures than about the heavenly Word made flesh, forgive us, O Lord.** Accept our thanks for the eternal gift conceived out of Your love for the world. **Accept our thanks, O Lord, for bringing the knowledge of this divine truth to us.**

Bless, O Lord, the musicians, singers, and messengers who help us rejoice in Your Son's birth. **Bless the reception of this Good News in the hearts of those who hear it.** Bless, O Lord, the spread of the Christmas message throughout the world. **May these glad tidings bring hope to the discouraged and peace to the troubled.** May the lonely see in the Christmas message the assurance of Your presence.

(*Here special intercessions, silent or spoken, may be made. If spoken, each portion concludes:* Lord, in Your mercy, **hear our prayer.**)

May the peace of Christmas fill our nation and the nations of the world. **This we ask in the name of our Savior, Christ, the Lord. Amen**

FIRST SUNDAY AFTER CHRISTMAS

O Lord our God, we praise You with our whole heart. **You have sent redemption to all people in the form of the Babe of Bethlehem.** You have revealed Your steadfast love by sending a Savior. **When the time was right, You sent Your Son, born of a virgin, so that all who believe in Him might receive adoption as Your children and become heirs to Your salvation.** Our hearts are filled with joy and gladness that by grace through faith in Jesus Christ we can now call You our Father.

We confess, dear Father, that we are unworthy of this, the greatest of all Your gifts. To be released from the slavery of sin, to become Your sons and daughters is beyond our understanding. **Marveling at Your great work, we recognize the gift of Your Son as undeniable proof of Your love toward us.** We thank You for calling Him into Egypt in His infancy so that He could grow up as our brother and bring us salvation through His death and resurrection.

Direct us, who know this infant Christ as our Savior, sanctify us, and govern us by Your Holy Spirit. Use us to bring Christ to the world's attention so that many others may experience Your divine goodness.

(Here special intercessions, silent or spoken, may be made. If spoken, each portion concludes: Lord, in Your mercy, **hear our prayer.**)

May the spirit of peace on earth and good will toward men linger with us now and in the days to come. **Make us the instruments of Your peace and good will toward all people.** This we ask in the name of the Lord of lords and King of kings, **Jesus Christ, our Savior. Amen**

SECOND SUNDAY AFTER CHRISTMAS

O God and Father of our Lord Jesus Christ, who has blessed us with every spiritual blessing in Christ, **we praise and adore You for choosing us in Him before the foundation of the world.** We cannot understand how this is possible, but we believe it because of the clear testimony of Your Word. **You destined us in love to be Your children through Christ, according to the purpose of Your will.**

You have chosen us, O Lord, that we should be holy and blameless before You. **Because of the weakness of our flesh, however, we are unable to achieve Your purpose.** But thanks be to You, for through Your Son Jesus Christ You have made us holy and blameless. **He took upon Himself our flesh and dwelt among us.** He has revealed Your glory as a light shining in the darkness. **From His fullness of glory we have received Your grace.** Now we know that we can stand before You in His righteousness. **For this, Your grace and mercy, accept our humble thanks.**

As You sent John the Baptist to point to the Light, which shines in the darkness, so also empower us with Your Spirit to bear witness to that Light. **You have given us power to receive Him, to believe in His name, and thereby to become Your children.** For the grace and truth we have received through Him, **we give You humble thanks.**

(*Here special intercession, silent or spoken, may be made. If spoken, each portion concludes:* Lord, in Your mercy, **hear our prayer.**)

In the name of Him whose light still shines to all the world for the salvation of many, **we pray. Amen**

THE EPIPHANY OF OUR LORD

Dear heavenly Father, in the darkness of this world's spiritual night, You created a special star to guide the Wise Men to Your Son. **For this revelation of Your glory, we give You humble thanks.** For predicting this event through your prophet Isaiah, hundreds of years before it took place, **we praise and adore You.**

Like Herod, we have often been guilty of being insincere in our search for Christ. **Forgive us, O Lord.** We have often failed to show others the way to Him, who is the Truth and the Light. **Have mercy on us, O Lord.** We confess that we have not always permitted Your Son to be the Light of our life. **Forgive us, O Lord.**

For guiding Gentiles to the birthplace of Your Son Jesus and for accepting their worship as fellow heirs and partakers of the promise in Christ Jesus through the Gospel, **we give You thanks.** For making it possible for us to become Your children through Christ, **we are eternally grateful.**

Send us Your Holy Spirit that He may increase our understanding of the magnitude of Your love. **Loosen our tongues and give us courage to tell the Good News to a world still largely in darkness.** Motivate us to generosity in bringing our gifts for the extension of Your kingdom. **Extend Your healing hand to the sick and Your presence to the lonely.**

(*Here special intercessions, silent or spoken, may be made. If spoken, each portion concludes:* Lord, in Your mercy, **hear our prayer.**)

Grant all governments sincere, honest, and wise officials. **We bring these our petitions in the name of Jesus Christ, our Lord and Savior. Amen**

THE BAPTISM OF OUR LORD
First Sunday after the Epiphany

Almighty and gracious God, Creator and Judge of all people, Father of our Lord Jesus Christ, **we praise You for Your concern to establish justice on the earth.** We thank You for sending Your Servant, our Lord Jesus Christ, to bring justice to all nations. **We thank You for identifying Him as your beloved Son by anointing Him with the Holy Spirit and power at His baptism.** For revealing Yourself as the Triune God at the baptism of our Lord, **we give You humble and hearty thanks.**

We confess, O Lord, that we have no righteousness of our own. **We are truly thankful that in our baptism You have given us forgiveness, life, and salvation.** For forgetting the significance of our baptism, **forgive us, O Lord.** For not measuring up to our high calling as Your sons and daughters, **we ask Your forgiveness.** We do not appeal to Your justice for what we deserve, but we appeal to Your mercy. **Have mercy on us, Lord.**

As You anointed Your Son with the Holy Spirit and power, help us remember that in our own baptism we received the gift of the Holy Spirit. **Through Him we have the power to believe Your Holy Word and receive the baptized Christ as our Savior.** Help us to establish and maintain justice on earth.

(*Here special intercessions, silent or spoken, may be made. If spoken, each portion concludes:* Lord, in Your mercy, **hear our prayer.**)

Grant that all people may hear the Good News that in Jesus Christ there is peace. **This we ask in the name and for the sake of Jesus Christ, our Lord and Savior. Amen**

SECOND SUNDAY AFTER THE EPIPHANY

Heavenly Father, eternal God, in whom alone is the power, the kingdom, and the glory, **hear the prayers of Your people as we come to You in the name of our Lord Jesus Christ.** We give You humble and hearty thanks that You have visited us by sending Your Son to be the Lamb of God who takes away the sin of the world. **Without Him we would be lost and condemned, but with Him we now have salvation.** For this Your undeserved kindness, we are eternally grateful.

We, who trust in Your Son as the Lamb of God, confess that we have not been a light to the nations as You expect. For failing to be such a light, **forgive us, O Lord.** For the times we have strayed from following in the steps of our Savior, **forgive us, O Lord.**

Help us to realize that by sharing our blessings with the poor, we thereby serve You. **Bless the councils of nations so that they may find ways to feed the world's hungry.** Use us to meet not only their physical needs, but also their spiritual needs. **May Your Holy Spirit move many more hearts to accept the invitation to come and see the promised Messiah.**

(*Here special intercessions, silent or spoken, may be made. If spoken, each portion concludes:* Lord, in Your mercy, **hear our prayer.**)

May the sick feel the power of Your healing; the disturbed in soul and mind, the tranquility of Your peace; and the lonely, the companionship of Your presence. **According to Your will grant our requests for Jesus' sake. Amen**

THIRD SUNDAY AFTER THE EPIPHANY

Dear heavenly Father, Lord of our life and Source of our salvation, we come before You with praise and adoration. **You have brought us from darkness into light and replaced our fear with faith.**

Yet, in spite of Your kindness and mercy, O Lord, we are guilty of giving offense. **We have too readily taken sides in religious issues that have been promoted by men.** We have often given offense to the Christian world by following people rather than our Lord Jesus Christ. **Forgive us, O Lord.** Heal the wounds that have been caused by our misguided words and actions. **Send Your Holy Spirit to motivate all hearts who claim You as Lord to walk in peace, harmony, and unity.** Use us, O Lord, to eliminate those divisions within Your body, the Church, which hinder the mission of winning the world for Christ. **Help us to keep the unity of the Spirit in the bond of peace.**

Help us, O Lord, to concentrate on our mission of being fishers of men. **Give us the spirit of sacrifice, which places the physical and spiritual needs of others above our own conveniences.** Be a light to those in darkness, and guide our feet into the paths of peace.

(*Here special intercessions, silent or spoken, may be made. If spoken, each portion concludes:* Lord, in Your mercy, **hear our prayer.**)

Continue to bless our nation with religious liberty, and curb the spread of crime and oppression. **Grant peace to the world that we may not be deterred from fulfilling Your Great Commission. We pray in Jesus' name. Amen**

FOURTH SUNDAY AFTER THE EPIPHANY

Lord God, almighty, eternal Judge of heaven and earth, we, Your unworthy servants, approach Your throne in earnest supplication. **We boast not of our own righteousness, for we have none that counts before Your holy demands.** But we come to You clothed in the merits of Your Son Jesus Christ.

We have not always walked in the counsel of the righteous nor delighted in Your law. Our pride has often prevented us from being poor in spirit and from receiving Your comfort when we mourn. **We have great difficulty in being meek when the world about us rewards those who are aggressive.** We have sought to quench our physical thirst instead of thirsting after Your righteousness. **We have expected mercy without being merciful, and we have blurred our vision with impurities.** We have often sown seeds of discord when we should have sought peace. **We have become irritated when others maligned us and have failed to rejoice when given an opportunity to suffer in Your behalf.** All this we have done and left undone and then wondered why our happiness was not complete. **For these and other departures from Your will, forgive us, O Lord.**

Help us, O Lord, to recognize Your mercy in calling us into Your service. **O Lord, You have chosen us and are the Source of our life.** May Your grace not be shed on us in vain, and may our lives reflect Your goodness.

(*Here special intercessions, silent or spoken, may be made. If spoken, each portion concludes:* Lord, in Your mercy, **hear our prayer.**)

Preserve us in faith until we come to the eternal day, **through Jesus Christ, our Lord. Amen**

FIFTH SUNDAY AFTER THE EPIPHANY

Lord God, heavenly Father, we delight in Your righteousness, truth, and mercy. **Your ears are ever open to the cry of the needy, and Your eyes alert to the needs of the poor.** Your statutes remind us to share our bread with the hungry, our homes with the homeless, and our clothing with the naked. **For the clarity of Your laws and the generosity of Your promises, we give You humble and hearty thanks.**

You desire that we, Your children, be the salt of the earth and the light of the world. **We confess, O Lord, that we do not measure up to Your expectations.** We have often failed to let the light of our faith shine to Your honor and glory. **Nor have we always been the cleansing salt in our society.** We have pointed accusing fingers at those who commit violence, while failing to recognize that the hatred in our hearts is just as abhorrent to Your righteousness. **We have tried to make peace with You before being reconciled with brother or sister, mother or father, son or daughter.** In the name of our compassionate Savior, we beg forgiveness.

By the power of Your Holy Spirit enable us to overcome our reluctance to share our abundance with others. Guide the judgments and understanding of our president and legislators that they may correctly assess the needs of the world and establish policies to help alleviate the sufferings of humanity. **May our sick know the power of Your healing, and the lonely, the comfort of Your presence.**

(*Here special intercessions, silent or spoken, may be made. If spoken, each portion concludes:* Lord, in Your mercy, **hear our prayer.**)

May the spiritually hungry be fed with the Bread of heaven, and may the disheartened and the downcast hear the Gospel. **This we ask in the name of our compassionate Savior. Amen**

SIXTH SUNDAY AFTER THE EPIPHANY

With our whole heart we seek You, O Lord. **Let us not wander from Your commandments.** It is our sincere desire to walk in all Your ways and keep all Your precepts. **We would choose that life which keeps us close to You and assures us of Your blessings.**

And yet, O Lord, we know that no matter how much we sincerely try to follow Your will, we so often fail. **Outwardly it may appear that we keep Your laws, but You know that our thoughts are often far from You.** So often we permit the spirit of the world to govern our eyes, our hands, and our tongues. **Without Your Holy Spirit within us, Lord, we cannot carry out Your will.** For our failure to abide by all Your commandments in thought, word, and deed, **forgive us, O Lord.**

Accept our thanks for sending Your only-begotten Son, Jesus Christ; **in Him rests the hope of our salvation.** We claim His righteousness for our unrighteousness, His sinlessness for our sinfulness, and His death for our life. **We stand before You in His righteousness, believing that for His sake You will hear our prayers.**

Direct those who govern us that they may lead our nation on the path of Your commandments. **Help them, O Lord, to administer Your laws in justice and mercy.** Have compassion on the wayward, and give insight and understanding to both the governed and to those who govern. **Grant that the world, which You have created and redeemed, may live in peace and harmony.**

(*Here special intercessions, silent or spoken, may be made. If spoken, each portion concludes:* Lord, in Your mercy, **hear our prayer.**)

We pray in the name of Him who took upon Himself the punishment for our sins, **even Jesus Christ, our Lord. Amen**

SEVENTH SUNDAY AFTER THE EPIPHANY

We praise and adore You, O Lord, for Your goodness and mercy endures forever. **You are merciful and gracious, slow to anger and abounding in steadfast love.** You do not deal with us according to our sins, nor do You repay us according to our transgressions. **As high as the heavens are above the earth, so great is Your steadfast love toward those who fear You.** As far as the East is from the West, **so far do You remove our transgressions from us.**

In spite of Your grace toward us, we must confess that we often do not deal so graciously with others. **When our neighbor offends us, we tend to pay Him back in kind.** We often think that we must take judgment and justice into our own hands, especially when the offender is not one of Your followers. **For permitting our old evil nature to rise up within us and seek revenge, forgive us, O Lord.** For being friendly only to those who are friendly to us, **we ask Your forgiveness.**

Bless us with the gift of Your Holy Spirit, for only with His help can we please You with the deeds of our lives. **Keep us steadfast in the faith so that we may stand before You, clothed in the righteousness of Jesus Christ.**

Grant us a government that administers justice impartially. **Give strength to the infirm, peace to the distressed, and courage to the fainthearted.**

(*Here special intercessions, silent or spoken, may be made. If spoken, each portion concludes:* Lord, in Your mercy, **hear our prayer.**)

Help us to forgive those who offend us. **This we ask in the name of Jesus Christ, our Savior. Amen**

EIGHTH SUNDAY AFTER THE EPIPHANY

O Lord God, for You alone our souls wait in patient silence. **You are the Rock of our salvation and our Fortress; therefore, we shall not be greatly moved.** Although we may sometimes think You have forgotten us, **Your Word assures us that our names are engraved on the palms of Your hands.**

We confess, O Lord, that in spite of these assurances, we often betray a lack of trust in Your providence. **We are overly concerned about our physical comforts.** We spend a great deal of time and money on food and clothing. **We worry about how we will cope if faced with a smaller income or increasing expenses.** We often forget Your promise that, if we place Your kingdom first in our lives, all other things will be added to us. **We have tried to serve two masters and have discovered it is not possible.**

Send us Your Holy Spirit to renew us and enable us to live as good stewards of Your mysteries. **Help us to be concerned, first of all, with pleasing You, rather than people.** Keep us from judging others prematurely. **Grant us faithfulness in the work we do for You.**

When we have failed to live up to Your expectations, **forgive us, O Lord.** Make us instruments of Your peace and messengers of Your Gospel. **Bless our nation that it may retain the law of religious freedom and liberty.** Protect us from terrorism and anarchy. **Be a friend to the underprivileged and a source of comfort to all people.**

(*Here special intercessions, silent or spoken, may be made. If spoken, each portion concludes:* Lord, in Your mercy, **hear our prayer.**)

Into Your powerful hands we commend ourselves **as we pray in Jesus' name. Amen**

THE TRANSFIGURATION OF OUR LORD
Last Sunday after the Epiphany

Almighty God, Lawgiver and Redeemer of the human race, we come before You in awe and reverence. **Your laws have saved humanity from anarchy and chaos; Your statutes help preserve our existence on this earth.** For preserving Your precepts through Moses, Elijah, and Your Son Jesus Christ, **we give You most hearty thanks.**

We confess that, although You have made Your will known through the prophets and apostles and have preserved it to the present day, we have not sufficiently treasured Your law and Gospel. **We have transgressed Your law and neglected many opportunities to spread Your Gospel.** We have been guilty at times of doubting the divine revelation of Your Word. **We have often given our own interpretation before searching Your Word for clarification.** We have had itching ears, listening for new doctrines, the commandments of men. **For our lack of careful concern in determining Your will, forgive us, O Lord.**

Through Your beloved Son Jesus Christ You have revealed Your Word in the flesh. **Send us Your Holy Spirit that we may hear Him speaking to us in Your Word.** Give us the courage to hold high the light of Your Word to those who sit in darkness, **and bless the hearts of those who hear it.**

(*Here special intercessions, silent or spoken, may be made. If spoken, each portion concludes:* Lord, in Your mercy, **hear our prayer.**)

Accept our thanks for permitting us to bask in the light of Your truth, **and lead us one day into the presence of Him who is this world's Light. In His most holy name we pray. Amen**

ASH WEDNESDAY

O God, Father of our Lord Jesus Christ and also our dear Father, **we thank You for permitting us to begin another Lenten season.** We are again privileged to meditate upon the cross of Christ and its meaning for us. **You have graciously granted us another opportunity for our relationship to be strengthened with Him who died to save us from our sins.** For Your gracious love, which prompted You to punish Your Son for our sins, **we give You humble and hearty thanks.**

In spirit we appear before You in sackcloth and ashes. **Send us Your Holy Spirit that He may help us to be genuinely sorry for our sins.** Help us to withstand the temptations of permitting the pleasures of this life, the worries of the day, and the activities of our daily routine to interfere with our Lenten worship and observance. **Draw us to Your wounded side and bring healing to our souls.** Help us to be conquerors over every temptation that confronts us.

(*Here special intercessions, silent or spoken, may be made. If spoken, each portion concludes:* Lord, in Your mercy, **hear our prayer.**)

Grant to Your Church an awareness of its responsibility to bring the Good News to everyone in the community. **Graciously bestow on us Your Holy Spirit so we may bear witness to You as our Savior.** To this end bless our Lenten services. **Grant us faithful attendance, and open our eyes to the opportunities for bringing others.** Add Your blessing to the Lenten messages, and through them strengthen our faith in Jesus Christ as our Savior. **This we ask in Jesus' name. Amen**

FIRST SUNDAY IN LENT

O Lord, our Creator and Redeemer, we praise You for creating man in Your own image. **We praise You for giving Adam Your righteousness and true holiness.**

We deplore, however, the existence of Satan, who caused our first parents to fall into the sin of disobedience. **We deeply regret that Satan, using a product of Your creation, caused man, the crown of Your creation, to fall from grace.** We also deplore our actual sins, the sins we commit daily. **They are many and great, and we do indeed repent of them. Forgive us, O Lord.**

Since Satan's power is still great and we are an easy mark for his assaults, **we implore You to give us the strength to resist him.** Strengthen our will and graciously enable us to govern our flesh to do Your will. **Send us Your Holy Spirit to empower our hearts with the desire and joy to resist the old man within us.** As we observe the power of Satan rampant in our world, causing many to worship him as You would be worshiped, **we implore You to curb his power and bring to naught his distressing activity among us.**

We give You humble thanks that as our substitute Your Son Jesus Christ successfully overcame the devil. **Grant us such success so that our days upon the earth may be peaceful and joyful.**

(*Here special intercessions, silent or spoken, may be made. If spoken, each portion concludes:* Lord, in Your mercy, **hear our prayer.**)

In the name of Him who conquered the forces of evil for us, **even our Lord Jesus Christ, we earnestly pray. Amen**

SECOND SUNDAY IN LENT

O Lord God, our heavenly Father and the Father of Abraham, Isaac, and Jacob, we praise You for Your faithfulness. **You made a covenant with Abraham and kept it; through him You blessed all the nations of the earth.** You counted his faith for righteousness, and according to Your promise, You sent to the world Your beloved Son. **For this, Your gracious gift of life and light, we give You humble thanks.**

We admit that we often think our good works should be of some value in Your sight and that we should receive some credit for them. **We know from Your Word, however, that if we wish to be saved by keeping the Law, we have to keep it perfectly.** Because we have not done this, **we can only trust in Your grace and mercy, O Lord.** As You counted Abraham's faith as righteousness, so we trust that You will graciously credit Christ's perfect righteousness to our account through our faith in Him.

Send us Your Holy Spirit, O Lord, that He may help us drink of the water that leads to everlasting life. Cause us to walk by faith in Your promises, **and grant that others may be inclined to follow and so find in Jesus Christ the Water of Life that quenches thirst forevermore.**

(*Here special intercessions, silent or spoken, may be made. If spoken, each portion concludes:* Lord, in Your mercy, **hear our prayer.**)

May Your peace rest on us and all nations, and may all recognize in You and Your Son Jesus Christ a source of healing for their bodies and a source of hope for their souls. **May we realize Your presence among us as Your love draws us ever closer to our heavenly home. In Jesus' name we pray. Amen**

THIRD SUNDAY IN LENT

Lord God, heavenly Father, we give You thanks for calling us out of darkness into Your marvelous light. **For the gift of sight, which enables us to see Your wonderful works of creation, we give You thanks.** For the faith by which we believe in Your Son Jesus Christ as our Savior, **we praise and adore You.**

We admit, O Lord, that we have not always used these gifts to the greatest advantage of Your kingdom. **We have seen the needs of others and failed to respond.** Our physical sight enables us to read Your Word; yet we have not used every opportunity to do so. **Our spiritual insight enables us to know Your will, and yet we have often acted contrary to Your commandments.** Our conscience condemns us for neglecting to do good when we have had the opportunity. **We have often impaired our vision by exposing ourselves to scenes and mental images that do not glorify You.** For closing our eyes to the needs of others and for failing to see the needs of Your kingdom, **forgive us, O Lord.**

May Your Holy Spirit enlighten us to the mysteries of Your Word. **Give us clear insight that we may confidently lead others into Your light.** Bless our efforts to enlighten the world with the truth of Your Gospel, and keep the light of faith burning brightly in our hearts. **Use us to alleviate the sufferings of the sick, and make us guides to the blind.**

(*Here special intercessions, silent or spoken, may be made. If spoken, each portion concludes:* Lord, in Your mercy, **hear our prayer.**)

Bless our leaders with insight to understand the needs of our nation and the world. **This we ask in Jesus' name. Amen**

FOURTH SUNDAY IN LENT

Lord God, our Father in heaven, the Source of our hope, light, and truth, accept our praise for Your divine providence. **We come to Your altar, rejoicing, because we know that Your merciful ears are open to our prayers through Jesus Christ, our Lord.**

According to Your law we stand condemned for our many transgressions. **We have often lived according to our flesh rather than setting our minds on the things of the Spirit.** Our souls have often been disquieted and cast down within us. **For failure to live hopefully with confidence in Your wisdom and might, forgive us, O Lord.** We have often been disturbed when others have been given preference in the affairs of Your kingdom. **We have failed to remember that greatness in Your kingdom is determined on the basis of service rather than preference.** For these and many other sins, **forgive us, O Lord.**

Send us Your Holy Spirit to guide us into Your truth. **Do not allow us to take offense with Christ because He was mocked, scourged, and crucified,** but give us His spirit of sacrifice and service. **Keep us from pride and envy.** Help us to overcome our natural desires toward things of the flesh, and set our minds on the things of the Spirit. **Give hope to the hopeless, healing to the sick, and the assurance of Your presence to the lonely.**

(*Here special intercessions, silent or spoken, may be made. If spoken, each portion concludes:* Lord, in Your mercy, **hear our prayer.**)

May the words of our mouths and the meditations of our hearts **be acceptable to You, O Lord, our Strength and Redeemer. Amen**

FIFTH SUNDAY IN LENT

Lord God, heavenly Father, whose Spirit gives us life, we magnify Your holy name. **Because You have heard our supplications and inclined Your ear to our prayers, we will call upon You as long as we live.** When we are brought low, You raise us up; You keep our eyes from tears and our feet from stumbling. **Therefore we will walk in Your ways as long as we are in the land of the living.**

It is our most earnest desire, O Lord, that Your Holy Spirit dwell within us. **Having become Your children through Christ, lead us by Your Spirit and help us to put to death the deeds of the flesh.** Graciously enable us to live as Your children and heirs, without fear. **When we are called upon to suffer for Your sake, remind us of the glory promised to those who permit the Spirit to lead them.** In the hour of trial, help us to remember that the sufferings of this present time are not worth comparing with the glory that is to be revealed to us.

When our hearts are burdened with the sorrow of losing a loved one, comfort us with the assurance of a blessed reunion in heaven. Grant that we may be among those who will be raised to everlasting life through faith in Jesus Christ.

Lord Jesus Christ, as You raised Lazarus from the dead, so remove from us the fear of death. Increase our faith and trust in You and remind us that temporal death is but the door to a glorious life that shall have no end. **Grant Your blessing to our efforts in bringing all our loved ones to this understanding and faith.**

(*Here special intercessions, silent or spoken, may be made. If spoken, each portion concludes:* Lord, in Your mercy, **hear our prayer.**)

In the name of Him who is the Resurrection and the Life, **even Jesus Christ, our Lord and Savior, we pray. Amen.**

PALM SUNDAY
Sunday of the Passion

With loud hosannas we come before You, O Lord of hosts. **We praise You for sending us Your Son as the King who came in Your name to establish peace between heaven and earth.** We are thankful that He did not consider Himself too far above us to become true man. **We deeply appreciate His fulfillment of the law, which we are unable to keep.** We cannot adequately express our thanks that Christ took our punishment upon Himself by dying on the cross.

Lord Jesus Christ, we confess that we have not always been faithful to our calling as Your chosen people. The deeds of our lives have often not matched the confession of our lips. **We have often broken communications with You by neglecting prayer, by failing to study Your Word, and by irregular attendance at Your Table.**

Because we know, O Lord, that You are merciful, **we dare to come before You, begging forgiveness.** May the assurance of that forgiveness, which we receive through Your Word and sacraments, **enable us to live lives of dedicated discipleship.**

Send us Your Holy Spirit to keep us on the path that leads to You. **Help us to withstand the temptations of Satan, the world, and our flesh.** Grant us grace to live to Your honor and glory **so that our lives will reflect our eternal gratitude for the salvation You won for us through Your life of perfect obedience and through Your sacrificial suffering and death.**

(*Here special intercessions, silent or spoken, may be made. If spoken, each portion concludes:* Lord, in Your mercy, **hear our prayer.**)

Grant peace in our time and help us maintain it; **we pray in the name of the King of kings and Lord of lords, Jesus Christ, our Savior. Amen**

MAUNDY THURSDAY

Lord God, heavenly Father, Author of the everlasting covenant and Giver of the cup of salvation, **we Your children gather in Your courts to offer our sacrifice of thanksgiving.** For fulfilling Your promise to establish a new covenant through the blood of Your Son Jesus Christ, **we give You humble and hearty thanks.** Through the veil of His flesh **we enter the Holy of Holies of Your presence without fear or trembling.** As our Lord Jesus Christ gave thanks to You when He broke the bread, **so we give You thanks.** As He gave thanks when He took the cup, **so we give You thanks.**

Lord Jesus Christ, both our High Priest and the Offering, **awe and wonder fill our hearts as we partake of Your body, broken for us, and Your blood, shed for us.** In our poverty of righteousness we have nothing to offer but our sins and gratitude. **Except for Your tremendous sacrifice we would still be in our sins.** But thanks be to You, for through Your Sacrament of the New Testament **we are assured that our iniquities are forgiven and our sins are no longer remembered.**

O Holy Spirit, dwell within us as we remember in this Sacrament our Lord's death. **Enter our hearts and help us to show our gratitude by encouraging one another to love and good works.**

(*Here special intercessions, silent or spoken, may be made. If spoken, each portion concludes:* Lord, in Your mercy, **hear our prayer.**)

Help us to live our lives as sacrifices of thanksgiving to Him who first loved us. **May our love for Him express itself in love and service to one another. In His name we pray. Amen**

GOOD FRIDAY

Lord God, heavenly Father, this day marks the anniversary of Your greatest gift to the world. **Your love for the human race is beyond our understanding.** We praise You for that love, which caused You to give up Your only-begotten Son unto death for sinful humanity. **Cleansed of our sin and clothed in His righteousness, we can now stand in Your presence.** We thank You for making us the beneficiaries of Your love in Christ.

O Lord Jesus Christ, we will never know the full extent of Your suffering for us. Because You asked Your Father to forgive those who put You on the cross, we know that our sins have also been forgiven. **Because You promised the criminal who believed in You everlasting life,** we have the assurance that, in spite of our sins, we too may have eternal life. **As in the midst of Your suffering You had consideration for Your mother,** so we can be confident You will be with us to the end of our earthly life. **Because You were forsaken by God the Father,** we know that we shall never be forsaken. **Because You thirsted for us,** we now have the water of everlasting life. **Because of Your declaration that the work of redemption was finished,** we no longer need to be doubtful about our salvation. **Through Your yielding up Your spirit to death,** we have life.

O Holy Spirit, abide in our hearts. Help us to believe that Christ died in our place. **Grant us a faith that bears testimony to our friends and community that this salvation is also available to them.**

(*Here special intercessions, silent or spoken, may be made. If spoken, each portion concludes:* Lord, in Your mercy, **hear our prayer.**)

So fill us with Your Holy Spirit that our lives will be a constant witness to our faith in the crucified Christ. **This we ask in the name of Jesus Christ, our Lord and Savior. Amen**

THE RESURRECTION OF OUR LORD
Easter Day

O God of life and Father of our Lord Jesus Christ, according to Your abundant grace, **You have begotten us again unto a new and living hope by the resurrection of Jesus from the dead.** You have transformed the night of doubt and sorrow into the new and eternal day of joy and gladness. **You have brought life and immortality to light by the glad tidings that Christ is risen. For this, O Lord, we give You thanks.** You have delivered Your Son, who died for our sins, from the grip of death and raised Him by Your power. **That which You sowed in dishonor and weakness, You raised in power and glory.** O God, we praise You that through Him You removed death's sting for us. **You have brought us victory over the grave.**

Fill our hearts with the joy of the resurrection. **Grant to Your Church the power of the resurrected Christ.** Help us to show forth Your praises. **Bless our homes with the comfort and hope of Easter.** Send the conquering banner of Christ's victory into all the world. **Grant that many more nations may join the hosts of heaven in songs of triumph.**

In the promise of Easter take away from us all fear of death. **Let the radiant beams of Easter's light shine into the depths of our souls.** Renew us in the Spirit of Him who is the Way, the Truth, and the Life. **Speak peace to our souls and maintain our faith in Him who promises resurrection and life.** Visit with Your divine presence those who are lonely.

(*Here special intercessions, silent or spoken, may be made. If spoken, each portion concludes:* Lord, in Your mercy, **hear our prayer.**)

Heal the sick and give courage to the disheartened. **We ask this in the name of our risen Lord. Amen**

SECOND SUNDAY OF EASTER

We give thanks to You, O Lord; we call upon Your name and sing praises to You for Your wonderful works. **By Your great mercy we have been born anew to a living hope through the resurrection of Jesus Christ from the dead.** Although we have not seen Him, we love Him. **We believe in Him and rejoice with inexpressible joy.**

We live in a scientific age, O Lord, and we like to see tangible evidence to support what we believe. **Forgive us, Lord, for being slow to accept the truth of Your Son's resurrection from the dead.** We are like Thomas, wanting to put our fingers into the nail prints of His hands and to thrust our hand into the wound of His side. **We often forget Christ's promise that, if we believe without seeing, we will be blessed even more than Thomas.** O Lord, we believe; **help our unbelief!**

Without the gift of Your Holy Spirit we cannot acknowledge Jesus Christ as our risen Lord. **Therefore, send us Your Holy Spirit that with steadfast hearts we may believe and always hold fast to the truth of our Savior's resurrection.** May the knowledge of Christ's resurrection from the dead reassure us of our own resurrection so that we can face temporal death without fear. **Take away all our doubts and cause us to believe that Jesus Christ is Your Son so that, believing, we may have eternal life in His name.**

(*Here special intercessions, silent or spoken, may be made. If spoken, each portion concludes:* Lord, in Your mercy, **hear our prayer.**)

This we ask in the name of Him who suffered and died in our place **and rose again from the dead for our justification, even our risen Lord and Savior Jesus Christ. Amen**

THIRD SUNDAY OF EASTER

Almighty God, whose power raised Jesus Christ from the dead, accept our thanks and praise for Your mighty act. **We thank You that You did not permit Your Holy One to see corruption in the grave, but through Him have made known to us the way of life.** For the evidence of so many eyewitnesses to His resurrection, **we give You thanks.**

O Lord, our lines have fallen for us in pleasant places and we have a goodly heritage. **The powerful truth of Your Son's resurrection has been handed down from generation to generation.** We believe not only because our parents believed, but because Your Holy Spirit through the Gospel has convinced us of Your everlasting truth. **As the risen Lord opened the eyes of the Emmaus disciples to the Scriptures, so open our eyes to Your spiritual truth.**

Lord Jesus Christ, as You accepted the invitation of the Emmaus disciples, **we ask that You break bread also with us.** Abide with us, for the day of this world's history is far spent, and it will soon pass away into the night of oblivion. **We need Your presence every passing hour, for You alone have the bread of life.** You nourish not only our bodies, but also our souls. **Help us to share Your physical and spiritual bread with others.**

(*Here special intercessions, silent or spoken, may be made. If spoken, each portion concludes:* Lord, in Your mercy, **hear our prayer.**)

By Your grace forgive us our sins and keep us in the faith. **May we one day experience Your presence, where there is fullness of joy and pleasure forevermore. Amen**

FOURTH SUNDAY OF EASTER

Lord God, heavenly Father, we, Your wandering sheep, gather in Your courts today. **Accept our praise for nourishing us in the green pastures of Your Word.** For leading us beside the still waters of Your forgiveness, we give You thanks. **You have restored our souls by leading us in the paths of Christ's righteousness.** For Your goodness and mercy, which follows us all the days of our life, **we give You thanks.**

And yet, O Lord, in spite of Your goodness and mercy, we have often strayed from the paths of righteousness. **We have failed to pass on that same goodness and mercy to others.** We lack patience in bearing the sufferings we bring upon ourselves by our own errors in judgment. **Not only have we been impatient with ourselves, but we have also been critical and impatient with others.** We have not learned to suffer patiently, especially when that suffering has come upon us unjustly. **We often forget that Christ suffered unjustly for our sins.** We have often struck back in word and deed against those who have mistreated us. **For these and many other sins, too numerous to mention, forgive us, O Lord.**

Send Your Holy Spirit, O Lord, to strengthen our faith. **May He help us recognize that Jesus Christ is the only door into Your kingdom.** Help us to believe that He is the only source of an abundant life both here and hereafter. **Help us to realize that the abundant life consists not only in things we possess, but also in the treasures You have stored up for us in Your kingdom.**

(*Here special intercessions, silent or spoken, may be made. If spoken, each portion concludes:* Lord, in Your mercy, **hear our prayer.**)

Bless our leaders in church and state and cause them to carry out Your will. **Grant our petitions in the name of Him who is the entrance door to Your divine majesty. Amen**

FIFTH SUNDAY OF EASTER

We rejoice in You, O Lord, and bring You our praises. **Your mercies are new every morning; daily You put a new song in our hearts.** Everywhere we look we see evidence of Your love and faithfulness. **We stand in holy awe as we consider Your wonderful works of creation.**

One of the greatest of Your works, O Lord, is the creation of Your Church, built upon the apostles and prophets, with Your Son Jesus Christ the Chief Cornerstone. **We acknowledge the undeserved love You have shown by calling us a chosen race, a royal priesthood, a holy nation.** You have called us out of darkness into Your marvelous light that we might declare Your wonderful works. **Once we were not a people, but now we are the people of God, and for this we give You thanks.**

And yet, O Lord, we confess that we have not always lived as Your people. **We have often taken too much pride in the fact that we are a chosen race, tending to look down on those who are not of our faith.** As a royal priesthood, we have not always been faithful in making intercessions for others. **Without the righteousness of Christ we certainly do not measure up to being a holy nation.** Forgive us, O Lord, for not living as people who have obtained Your mercy.

In spite of our failures, O Lord, we take comfort in the promise of Your Son Jesus Christ that He has prepared heavenly mansions for those who trust in Him as the Way, the Truth, and the Life.

(Here special intercessions, silent or spoken, may be made. If spoken, each portion concludes: Lord, in Your mercy, **hear our prayer.**)

In the name of Him who is the Resurrection and the Life, **even Jesus Christ, our Savior, we pray. Amen**

SIXTH SUNDAY OF EASTER

O Lord God Almighty, You are remembered by Your great deeds in the history of the human race. **In times of trouble You delivered Your chosen people from the hands of their enemies.** Through Your Son Jesus Christ You relieved many of their physical and spiritual ills. **For Your great power, displayed both in the past and in the present, accept our glorious praise.**

We confess, O Lord, that we have not always extolled Your name among our fellow citizens. **The results of Your power among us have given us hope in our trials and tribulations.** Even so, we have often failed to give an account to others for the reason of the hope that is within us. **We rejoice in Your mercy, which gives us the assurance of the forgiveness of our sins through our Lord Jesus Christ.** Being righteous, He gave His life for us, the unrighteous. **You have merited our love; yet we have failed to show our love by keeping Your commandments.** For our failure to show You proper love and reverence, forgive us, O Lord.

Send us Your Holy Spirit that He may help us to express our love to You in word and deed. May He abide within us that we may walk in newness of life.

May the lonely experience Your presence, and the sick Your healing. May the fainthearted be filled with courage to extol Your name.

(*Here special intercessions, silent or spoken, may be made. If spoken, each portion concludes:* Lord, in Your mercy, **hear our prayer.**)

We ask these petitions in the name of Him who is the Resurrection and the Life, **even Jesus Christ, our Savior. Amen**

THE ASCENSION OF OUR LORD

O Lord Jesus Christ, exalted far above all principalities, power, might, and dominion, at whose name every knee should bow, not only in this world but also in the world to come, **accept our praise and adoration.**

We know that our praise cannot exalt You any higher than the position You already have at the right hand of God the Father, **yet we are bold enough to believe that You delight in the commendation of Your children.** Accept our humble thanks for giving us the privilege of being part of Your body, the Church.

For the many appearances You made after Your resurrection, proving to witnesses that You had risen from the dead, we are grateful. We also thank You for assembling so many of the faithful to witness Your ascension. **These witnesses to Your resurrection and ascension inspire us to follow You.**

As the ascended Head of the Church, O Lord, You are aware of the many problems confronting the Church today. **We do not ask that our work be made easier, but only for Your power to help us cope with the problems.** Help us to be Your hands, doing deeds of kindness. **Help us to be Your feet, running errands of mercy.** Help us to be Your mouth, witnessing to Your love and salvation.

(*Here special intercessions, silent or spoken, may be made. If spoken, each portion concludes:* Lord, in Your mercy, **hear our prayer.**)

When at last we have fulfilled Your purpose in our lives, **take us to Your ascension throne, where we may share Your glory forevermore. Amen**

SEVENTH SUNDAY OF EASTER

We sing Your praises, O Lord Most High. **As nations battle each other, we know that You are still in control of the universe.** To know that You rule over all the earth and determine the destiny of all people gives us confidence and assurance. **Accept our songs of praise, O Lord Most High.**

You have exalted Your Son Jesus Christ to the right hand of Your majesty. **We praise You for His ascension and His exaltation.** Since He is no longer physically present among us, we implore You to help us become **His hands to administer to our fellowmen,** His feet to extend Your kingdom to the uttermost parts of the world, **and His tongue to speak the message of Your Gospel.** The mission You have assigned to us seems impossible because of our human frailties; **we are dependent upon Your help to fulfill Your purposes.**

As Christ's first disciples were promised power through the Holy Spirit to accomplish this mission, **so we believe that Your promise through Christ also extends to us.** The growth of Your Church through the centuries is evidence of Your power in all generations. **Therefore with confidence and trust we now ask You to grant us that same power.** Through Your Holy Spirit use us in the service of Your kingdom.

(*Here special intercessions, silent or spoken, may be made. If spoken, each portion concludes:* Lord, in Your mercy, **hear our prayer.**)

Grant, O Lord, that, as we proclaim the Gospel of salvation, we may, at the same time, be a unifying influence in all Christendom. **In Jesus' name we pray. Amen**

PENTECOST

Lord God, heavenly Father, Creator of all things great and small, **we, Your creatures, come before You, our hearts filled with gratitude and praise.** As we consider the complexity of the smallest living being and give thought to the marvelous way in which You have made us, **we stand in awe of Your wisdom.** Not only have You marvelously created all things, but You have also provided for their continuing needs; **You open Your hands, and they are filled with good things.** For this Your care and providence, **we give You humble thanks.**

Since we live by the breath of Your mouth and our souls need nourishment as well as our bodies, **we are especially thankful on this day of Pentecost that You poured out the gift of Your Holy Spirit.** By His power we have become Your children through faith in Jesus Christ. **As Your children we need constant renewal and strengthening of our faith.** We claim Your promise, given through Your prophet Joel, that You would pour out Your Spirit on all flesh, **and we implore You to include us in the fulfillment of that promise.**

As members of Your Church, **we ask You to give us the wisdom and the dedication to carry out our awesome responsibility for the welfare of souls and the upbuilding of Your kingdom.**

(*Here special intercessions, silent or spoken, may be made. If spoken, each portion concludes:* Lord, in Your mercy, **hear our prayer.**)

In the name of the Head of the Church, **even our Lord Jesus Christ, we pray. Amen**

THE HOLY TRINITY
First Sunday after Pentecost

God the Father, God the Son, and God the Holy Spirit, One in Three and Three in One, **accept our praise for our creation, redemption, and sanctification.**

Heavenly Father, Author of our creation, **we give You thanks for permitting us to live in Your beautiful world.** For the lofty skies, the warmth and energy of the sun, summer and winter, and day and night, **we give You thanks.** For the evidence of Your power, which is revealed in towering mountain peaks, ocean tides, the lightning of a storm, and mighty rushing winds, **we give You thanks.** For Your inestimable love, which provides for all our needs, and most of all for Your redemption of the world by our Lord and Savior Jesus Christ, **we give You thanks.**

O Jesus Christ, Author and Finisher of our faith, for redeeming us from the power of Satan, for freeing us from the slavery of sin, and for opening the gates of everlasting life, **accept our sincere gratitude.** For showing us how to live with people, for suffering and dying for us, for giving our lives a purpose by commissioning us to be Your witnesses, **accept our sincere gratitude.**

O Holy Spirit, Source of our faith, for calling us by the Gospel, for enlightening us with Your gifts, for establishing the Christian Church on earth, for keeping us in the true faith, **we give You thanks.**

O Father, Son, and Holy Spirit, in the midst of all Your blessings, **we have been guilty of abusing Your gifts.** We have been wasteful of Your created resources. **We have failed to carry out Your Great Commission. For all of this, forgive us, O Lord.**

(*Here special intercessions, silent or spoken, may be made. If spoken, each portion concludes:* Lord, in Your mercy, **hear our prayer.**)

All honor and glory, power and might, be to You, O Lord, **as we pray in the name of the Father, the Son, and the Holy Spirit. Amen**

SECOND SUNDAY AFTER PENTECOST

Lord God, heavenly Father, accept our thanks and praise for revealing Your will to us in Your law. **Experience has taught us that it is to our advantage to obey Your law,** for disobeying it only makes our lives miserable. **While we believe that obeying Your law brings blessings, we do not believe that keeping it can bring us any nearer to eternal life.**

All of us have sinned and fallen short of Your glory. **We should be more diligent in teaching Your will to our children,** but we make excuses for ourselves by saying we do not have time. **We neglect opportunities to speak about You when we are walking, when we retire, and when we greet the morning sun.** We pride ourselves that we do not sin as often or as flagrantly as others. **Yet our boasting is vain for even one sin makes us sinners.** Because of this, Lord, we have no place to turn except to Your mercy. **For the sake of Jesus Christ, our resurrected Lord, who shed His blood for the expiation of our sins, forgive us, O Lord.**

Help us, O Lord, to build our spiritual house on the solid foundation of Jesus Christ and His Word. **Through Your Holy Spirit strengthen our faith to endure the trials and sorrows of life.** Not only for ourselves, but also for our families and associates, with whom You have placed us, we pray:

(*Here special intercessions, silent or spoken, may be made. If spoken, each portion concludes:* Lord, in Your mercy, **hear our prayer.**)

Safeguard the freedoms and liberties protected by the laws of our land. **With faith in Jesus Christ, the only Source of our righteousness, we pray. Amen**

THIRD SUNDAY AFTER PENTECOST

Almighty God, everlasting Father, a present help in the day of trouble and a faithful listener to all our needs, **we, Your unworthy children, come before You dressed in the righteousness of our Savior Jesus Christ.** Accept our praise and thanksgiving for Your providence. **Your mercies are new every morning and Your mighty arm protects us every night.** For Your countless mercies **we give You thanks.**

We confess that we have many more fulfillments of Your promises to encourage us to believe in You than did Abraham, and yet we wait for Your answers impatiently. **You do not ask us to sacrifice our livelihood in order to follow You, yet, unlike Matthew, we hesitate to give up the little You ask.** We appreciate that You now call us Your children in Christ, yet our pride and security in such knowledge often causes us to depreciate others. **We claim to follow You, but often we do so at too great a distance.** We hesitate to get fully involved in the work of Your kingdom. **For our lack of zeal and wholeheartedness, forgive us, O Lord.**

Fill us with Your Holy Spirit that we may more fully believe Your promises. **Give us Your grace that we may show more love and mercy.** Strengthen us that we may follow You more closely, and help us to believe that our faith will be reckoned to us as righteousness.

(*Here special intercessions, silent or spoken, may be made. If spoken, each portion concludes:* Lord, in Your mercy, **hear our prayer.**)

This we ask in the name of and for the sake of Jesus Christ, **who considered Himself as a servant and associated with sinners. Amen**

FOURTH SUNDAY AFTER PENTECOST

Hear our praise, O Lord, and give ear to the voice of our supplications. **We enter Your gates with thanksgiving and Your courts with praise.** You are righteous and Your steadfast love abides forever. **We are Your people and the sheep of Your pasture.** We serve You with gladness and come into Your presence with singing.

Your blessings are too great for us to comprehend. We are unworthy of them for we have often broken the covenant You made with Your chosen people. **We have failed to live up to Your expectations of being a kingdom of priests and a holy nation.** You have shown us Your love by sending Jesus, the Christ, to die for us while we were yet sinners. **We have failed, however, to return that love which reconciled us to Yourself by His death and saved us by His life.** Furthermore, we have failed to share this knowledge of salvation with those who are as sheep without a shepherd. **For these and many other negligences, forgive us, O Lord.**

Send us Your Holy Spirit, O Lord, and strengthen us with Your presence. **Fill us with knowledge and zeal to do Your will.** Help us to teach Your Word, and fill us with compassion for those who have not yet received You as their Shepherd. **Open our eyes to the plenteous harvest, and make us willing laborers to gather it in.**

(*Here special intercessions, silent or spoken, may be made. If spoken, each portion concludes:* Lord, in Your mercy, **hear our prayer.**)

This we ask in the name of the Lord of the harvest, our Savior, **who reconciled us to Yourself by His death and saved us by His life, even Jesus Christ, our Lord. Amen**

FIFTH SUNDAY AFTER PENTECOST

O Lord God, Source of our strength and Refuge of the weary and misunderstood, **accept our praise for the assurance of Your presence; accept our thanks for Your concern.**

Lord we believe; help us to overcome our unbelief. **For taking offense when we feel others are putting us down, forgive us, O Lord.** For misunderstanding the attitudes of others, forgive us, O Lord. **For imagining evil intent against us when no evil is intended, forgive us, O Lord.** For plotting revenge on those who have abused us, forgive us, O Lord. **For forgetting that Your Son Jesus Christ bore the penalty for all our sins, we ask Your forgiveness.** For not remembering that in You we can find perfect justice, we ask Your forgiveness. **For sometimes feeling that even You have forsaken us, we ask Your forgiveness.**

To overcome our feelings of hostility, send us Your Holy Spirit. **To be more understanding of others, give us Your patience.** To deal with those who abuse us, give us the spirit of forgiveness. **To acknowledge You openly before the world, give us courage.**

Grant, O heavenly Father, peace to the nations of the world. **Subdue the ungodly who are warring unjustly against other nations.** Use us to help the refugees and the hungry. **Give wisdom and good judgment to the president of our nation, to our governors, the congress, and state legislators.**

(*Here special intercessions, silent or spoken, may be made. If spoken, each portion concludes:* Lord, in Your mercy, **hear our prayer.**)

Let there be loving concern between our church bodies and fellow Christians. **This we ask in the name of our Lord Jesus Christ. Amen**

SIXTH SUNDAY AFTER PENTECOST

We will extol Your steadfast love, O Lord, forever. **We will proclaim Your faithfulness to all generations.** Your faithfulness is as firm as the heavens; **Your righteousness is the glory of our strength.**

We give You thanks for calling us through our baptisms to be Your chosen ones. **Baptized into Christ's death, we renounced Satan and his wicked works** and rose from the death of sin to the newness of life. **But we have often failed to walk in newness of life. Forgive us, O Lord.** You have told us that if we are afraid to lose our life in Your service, we will not know the real meaning of the Christian life. **We have been afraid to risk our lives in the defense of Your kingdom.** For these and many others sins, **forgive us, O Lord.** You have told us that when we proclaim Your Gospel we may expect conflict. **Because we are afraid of conflict, we have often failed to proclaim Your Gospel in our homes and among our fellow people. Forgive us, O Lord.**

Remind us, by the continual visitation of Your Holy Spirit, to walk in newness of life. **May He also strengthen us to become more courageous in the presence of conflict.** Preserve our political and religious freedoms so that Your Gospel may have free course to extend Your kingdom.

(*Here special intercessions, silent or spoken, may be made. If spoken, each portion concludes:* Lord, in Your mercy, **hear our prayer.**)

May the Holy Spirit grant us the spiritual insight to see that only in the willingness to lose our life for Your sake, will we find it. **In Jesus' name we pray. Amen**

SEVENTH SUNDAY AFTER PENTECOST

We will praise You, our God and King, and bless Your name forever and ever. **You are faithful in all Your words and gracious in all Your deeds.** You uphold all who are falling and raise up all who are bowed down. **All eyes look to You for food in due season. You open Your hand and satisfy the desire of every living thing.**

O heavenly Father, we praise You especially for Your Son Jesus Christ, whom You sent as Your Messenger of peace. **We thank You that He fulfilled the words of the prophet by riding into the city of Jerusalem amid shouts of recognition that He was the Christ.** For the assurance that Jesus fulfilled the prophetic utterances regarding Him, **we give You thanks.**

We confess, O Lord, that although Your Word tells us that You sent Christ to bring peace to the nations, **we have often permitted the conflicts between nations to cause us to doubt Your Word.** For our shortsightedness, forgive us, O Lord. **You have not failed us, but we have failed You.** For failing to be zealous in the proclamation of Your Gospel, forgive us, O Lord. **We are weary of fighting the war of sin within ourselves, and we are disturbed by the violence and hatred we observe around us.** Forgive our inclinations toward giving up the fight. **We have given in to our own wills to do what we want rather than doing what You want. Forgive us, O Lord.**

(Here special intercessions, silent or spoken, may be made. If spoken, each portion concludes: Lord, in Your mercy, **hear our prayer.**)

In our weariness of the flesh grant us Your Holy Spirit to enable us to accept the invitation of Your Son to come to Him. **May we find in Him rest for our souls. Amen**

EIGHTH SUNDAY AFTER PENTECOST

O Lord God, almighty Creator, You spoke and the universe came into being. **By the exertion of Your will the earth was populated with herds and flocks.** By Your Word vegetation and grain sprang forth to nourish all living things. **We are grateful that Your power still exists among us.**

As the rain and the snow come down from heaven at Your command and nourish the earth, **so You have promised that Your mighty Word, sown as seed in the hearts of men, women, and children everywhere, will produce results.** Send Your Holy Spirit to prepare our hearts to receive Your Holy Word. **Prevent us from hardening our hearts so that Your Word cannot penetrate.** Keep us from short-lived emotional reaction to Your Word. **Protect us from the thorns of coveting, which are able to choke out our faith.** Make our hearts a fertile field so that Your Word may produce the fruits of faith a hundredfold.

As we sow the seed of Your Word on the hearts of many, may Your Holy Spirit bless it that it may spring forth into a lively hope. When, O Lord, we see little or no results of the Word we have spread, **encourage us to remain faithful sowers with Your promise that Your Word shall not return empty.**

Bless the administration of our government that it may help provide a healthy climate for the seed we sow to germinate and bring forth fruit.

(*Here special intercessions, silent or spoken, may be made. If spoken, each portion concludes:* Lord, in Your mercy, **hear our prayer.**)

This we ask in the name of the Lord of the harvest, **even Jesus Christ, our Lord and Savior. Amen.**

NINTH SUNDAY AFTER PENTECOST

Lord God, heavenly Father, we give thanks to You with our whole hearts. **We praise You for being gracious and merciful, slow to anger, and steadfast in love.** For teaching us Your way, O Lord, and for enabling us to walk in Your truth, **we give You thanks.**

Send us Your Holy Spirit that He may teach us how to pray. **Since words cannot express our innermost feelings, grant that the Holy Spirit intercede for us according to Your will.** May we know the mind of the Spirit. **Help us to trust that what we ask of You according to Your will, we will receive.**

Since, O Lord, You have entrusted the management of Your kingdom to us, **we ask Your guidance and insight to carry out our responsibilities in a manner acceptable to You.** Help us to be diligent in planting the seed of Your Word. **Preserve us from the enemies who would sow seeds of discord, disloyalty, and subversion of Your Word.** In our zeal to bring in the harvest, help us to be patient so that we do not jeopardize the good by pulling out the bad too quickly.

Be with our president, our governor, and the legislators of all levels of our government. Give hope for healing to the sick, encouragement to the discouraged, and the assurance of Your presence to the lonely.

(Here special intercessions, silent or spoken, may be made. If spoken, each portion concludes: Lord, in Your mercy, **hear our prayer.**)

We pray in the name of our Redeemer, **the First and the Last, the Eternal, our Lord Jesus Christ. Amen**

TENTH SUNDAY AFTER PENTECOST

Lord God, heavenly Father, we praise You for Your wonderful testimonials. **Your words give light and impart understanding to the simple.** For dealing with us according to Your steadfast love, **We give You thanks.**

In spite of Your steadfast love, O Lord, we have broken Your laws. **We complain about our short-sighted understanding and fail to pray for enlightenment.** We have often considered earthly wealth to be more valuable than knowledge of Your holy will. **We have thought lightly of the pearl of great price and neglected many of the treasures hidden in Your Word.** We have often failed to be zealous in casting out the net of Your Word to catch sinners for Your kingdom. **We worry about the adverse things that could happen to us and forget that all things work together for good to those who love You.** We are assured of our salvation through Your Son Jesus Christ, but we often fail to conform to His image. **For these and other transgressions against Your holy will, forgive us, O Lord.**

Help us with the guidance of Your Holy Spirit to choose that which is truly valuable in life. **Help us to arrange our priorities in accordance with that which will advance Your kingdom.** Give spiritual insight to our leaders in church and state, **that we may live our lives in quietness and good order.**

(Here special intercessions, silent or spoken, may be made. If spoken, each portion concludes: Lord, in Your mercy, **hear our prayer.**)

May Your presence be in our homes and nation. **This we ask in the name of Jesus Christ, our Lord and Savior. Amen**

ELEVENTH SUNDAY AFTER PENTECOST

Eternal Father, Lord of creation, Source of all our abundance, and answer to all our needs, **we, Your unworthy creatures, come before You with praise and thanksgiving.** You give all creatures their food in due season; **You open Your hand and satisfy the needs of every living thing.** You have made provisions for our souls by sending Your Son Jesus Christ as a token of Your love. **For all these physical and spiritual blessings we give You thanks.**

For a world suffering from persecution, famine, nakedness, peril, and war, we implore Your mercy. **Give us compassion for the hungry, and use us to alleviate their suffering.** As You miraculously fed the five thousand, so multiply our gifts that they may be sufficient to meet the desperate needs of many of our fellow human beings. **Make those involved in administering to the needs of the world careful managers of the resources available so that nothing is wasted.** Grant nations that have plenty a spirit of generosity towards those less fortunate. **Give assurance to those who are suffering that neither death nor life,** nor angels nor principalities, nor things present nor things to come, nor height nor depth, **nor anything else in all creation, will be able to separate them from the love of God in Christ Jesus our Lord.**

(*Here special intercessions, silent or spoken, may be made. If spoken, each portion concludes:* Lord, in Your mercy, **hear our prayer.**)

This we ask in the name of our compassionate Savior, **Jesus Christ our Lord. Amen**

TWELFTH SUNDAY AFTER PENTECOST

We give thanks to You, O Lord our God; **with our whole heart we glorify Your name forever.** With You there is righteousness and peace; **with You our land shall prosper.** Your steadfast love and faithfulness is our hope in an evil day.

We confess, O Lord, that, like Elijah, we too easily become discouraged. Most of what we hear and read about is bad news. **The many crimes against Your holy laws that we hear about and the many transgressions we see committed by those around us** often leave us wondering whether anyone is still serving You. **In our own lives we have also often failed to heed Your still small voice by which You attempt to guide us.** For our overemphasis of the negative aspects of Your kingdom and for forgetting the positive—**forgive us, O Lord.**

In the midst of the storms of this life we need the strength of Your Holy Spirit and the presence of Your Son Jesus Christ. **Send us Your Holy Spirit to keep our spiritual eyes focused on Jesus.** When the waves of trouble begin to engulf us and we feel ourselves sinking, **take our hands of faith, raise us above our doubts, and replace our fears with courage.** Protect our nation, O Lord, from enemies within and without and preserve Your Church in Your saving Word. **Be a source of hope for the discouraged.**

(*Here special intercessions, silent or spoken, may be made. If spoken, each portion concludes:* Lord, in Your mercy, **hear our prayer.**)

Be with the sick and the bereaved. **We pray in the name of Jesus Christ, our Lord. Amen**

THIRTEENTH SUNDAY AFTER PENTECOST

Lord God, heavenly Father, we, Your adopted children in Christ, have assembled in Your house of prayer. **We bring You our praise and adoration for accepting us as Your children through Jesus Christ, our Lord.** We thank You for graciously blessing us by extending to us the knowledge of salvation.

We confess that we are unworthy of Your saving power. We have not kept justice, nor have we acted righteously. **We have broken Your laws and profaned Your Sabbath; we have not kept Your holy covenant.** Because of our prejudices against those who are not of our own nationality, we have hindered the spread of the Gospel to many nations. **We have failed to share the crumbs that have fallen from the Master's table.** We have attempted to win Your favor with offerings and sacrifices. **For these and all our transgressions we ask Your forgiveness.**

Enliven us with Your Holy Spirit so that we may adequately express our gratitude and praise. **Move us to share not only the increase of the earth, but also Your saving power with other nations.** Help us to welcome the foreigner and the stranger in our midst and extend them the mercy that You have extended to us.

(*Here special intercessions, silent or spoken, may be made. If spoken, each portion concludes:* Lord, in Your mercy, **hear our prayer.**)

In the name of Him who proclaimed Your mercy to us, **even Jesus Christ, our Lord. Amen**

FOURTEENTH SUNDAY AFTER PENTECOST

In awe and wonder we appear before You, Lord God heavenly Father. **Your judgments are unsearchable and Your ways inscrutable.** We cannot understand why You chose Abraham, Isaac, and Jacob to be Your people. **Nor can we comprehend why You should be concerned about us, miserable offenders.** But we praise You for Your mercy and grace to the fallen children of men. **Accept our thanks for Your love, which reaches down from heaven and gives us salvation in Your Son Jesus Christ, our Lord.**

We confess, O Lord, that we have not always clearly identified Jesus Christ as Your Son. **The way we have used and not used the Office of the Keys leaves much to be desired.** We have not always shown the rocklike faith that should characterize those to whom You have given this power. **For our lack of zeal in proclaiming Jesus Christ as Your Son, forgive us, O Lord.** For our lack of good judgment in exercising the power You have given to Your Church in the Office of the Keys, forgive us, O Lord.

Send us Your Holy Spirit, O Lord, to give us good judgment in the affairs of Your kingdom. Grant us a firm faith in Jesus Christ, Your Son, our Savior. **Help us bring hope to the hopeless and peace to the restless.**

(Here special intercessions, silent or spoken, may be made. If spoken, each portion concludes: Lord, in Your mercy, **hear our prayer.**)

Enable us to forgive as we have been forgiven, and bless us with Your continual presence. **This we ask in the name of Jesus. Amen**

alternate:

We have failed to share the crumbs that have fallen from the Master's table. We have attempted to win Your favor with offerings and sacrifices. **For these transgressions we ask Your forgiveness.**

FIFTEENTH SUNDAY AFTER PENTECOST

O Lord our God, we come to You with hearts filled with gratitude and praise. **For the light of another day we give You thanks.** For making us Your children through Christ, we praise Your holy name. **For giving us Your Word as a source of our joy, accept our praise.**

We acknowledge, O Lord, that in spite of Your lovingkindness toward us, we have often brought discredit to Your holy name. **We have often failed in our worship by permitting ourselves to be conformed to this world.** We have not always demonstrated Your will in selecting that which is good, acceptable, and perfect. **We have often thought more highly of ourselves than we should.** We have often failed to exercise sober judgment according to our faith. **We sometimes forget that, while we are many members of Your body, we are one body in Christ.** Having gifts that differ according to the grace given to us, we have failed to use these gifts for the best interests of Your kingdom. **For these many neglects, forgive us, O Lord.**

Send us Your Holy Spirit that as members of Your body we may fulfill our purpose with greater zeal. **Remembering Your mercy toward us, may we be more merciful toward others.** Keep us united in the faith that we may carry out our responsibilities with greater cheerfulness. **Help us find meaning and joy in our lives by making us more willing to lose them in Your service.** Bless our nation with righteousness and peace, and use us to help alleviate the suffering of humanity.

(*Here special intercessions, silent or spoken, may be made. If spoken, each portion concludes:* Lord, in Your mercy, **hear our prayer.**)

We ask these petitions **in the name of and for the sake of Him who denied Himself so that He might save us. Amen**

SIXTEENTH SUNDAY AFTER PENTECOST

Lord God, heavenly Father, we begin another day of our lives secure in Your protection. **Accept our songs of praise.** For Your laws which curb the violence of the wicked, **we give You thanks.** For the security of family and friends, whose love we can depend on because they love You, **we sing Your praises.**

As beneficiaries of the order You have established for the well-being of the human race, we regretfully acknowledge our shortcomings. **We have frequently sidestepped Your command to warn the wicked.** By our disregard of Your constituted authority on earth, we have also failed to set a proper example. **Our transgressions against You and our neighbor indicate that our love leaves much to be desired. Forgive us, O Lord.**

Direct, sanctify, and govern our lives with Your Holy Spirit so that we may live to Your honor and glory and for the benefit of others. **Give wisdom, understanding, and insight to those who govern us.** Grant peace to our nation and to our world. **May the sick experience Your healing.** Give courage to the fainthearted, and assure the lonely of Your presence. **Bless the efforts of Your Church as it carries out its responsibilities of the Great Commission.** Curb the evil influence of Satan as he attempts to bring disunity in Your body, the Church.

(*Here special intercessions, silent or spoken, may be made. If spoken, each portion concludes:* Lord, in Your mercy, **hear our prayer.**)

According to Your promise that You will answer when two of us agree about anything for which we ask, **hear our prayer in Jesus' name. Amen**

SEVENTEENTH SUNDAY AFTER PENTECOST

With all that is within us, O Lord, we bless Your holy name. **You forgive all our iniquities and heal our diseases.** You redeem our life from destruction and crown us with lovingkindness and tender mercies. **For all these blessings, O Lord, we give You thanks.**

Your mercies remind us that we have not always treated others with the same undeserved love. **We expect constant forgiveness from others but count the times we forgive them.** We expect full payment from others while attempting to get discounts for ourselves. **We live too much for ourselves and not enough to Your honor and glory.** We become impatient with others but expect them to be patient with us. **We often forget that it's not up to us to settle all accounts, but that You have the power to bring good out of evil.** For these, our many transgressions, **forgive us, O Lord.**

By Your Spirit help us to reflect Your mercy toward others. **Make us confident that You will take our mistakes and turn them into blessings.** Be with the president, governor, and legislators, and help them to represent us in answering people's needs. **Be with the lonely, comfort the sick, and bring the assurance of Your forgiveness to the penitent.**

(*Here special intercessions, silent or spoken, may be made. If spoken, each portion concludes:* Lord, in Your mercy, **hear our prayer.**)

This we ask in the name of and for the sake of Him who taught us how to forgive, **even, Jesus Christ, our Lord and Savior. Amen**

EIGHTEENTH SUNDAY AFTER PENTECOST

O Lord, our Light and Salvation, You are the Stronghold of our life. **With You as our God, we face the world without fear.** As the heavens are high above the earth, so Your ways are higher than our ways and Your thoughts higher than our thoughts. **We behold Your beauty in the midst of Your sanctuary and dare to bring our petitions before You.**

We readily admit, O Lord, that our manner of life has not always been worthy of the Gospel. **We have not always stood firm in one spirit, with one mind striving side by side for the faith.** We have failed to work diligently in Your vineyard and have too readily adopted the standards of the world in desiring rewards for our labors. **For our lack of zeal to work in Your vineyard, forgive us, O Lord.** For begrudging Your favors to those who have worked less than we, **we ask Your forgiveness.** For forgetting that You have already paid us with the gift of salvation, **forgive us, O Lord.**

That we may be more enthusiastic about carrying out Your wishes, send us Your Holy Spirit. **Help us to see the opportunities to do Your work, and according to Your mercy, grant success to our labors.** Grant righteousness and peace to our nation and to the nations of the world. **Use us to comfort the lonely and bring hope to the sick and discouraged.**

(*Here special intercessions, silent or spoken, may be made. If spoken, each portion concludes:* Lord, in Your mercy, **hear our prayer.**)

Help us to feed the hungry and clothe the needy. **This we ask in the name of Jesus. Amen**

NINETEENTH SUNDAY AFTER PENTECOST

Lord God, heavenly Father, to You we lift up our souls, in You we put our trust. **We are mindful of Your mercies; throughout our lives You have shown us Your steadfast love.** You have provided for our eternal salvation by sending us Your Son Jesus Christ. **For these countless gifts of Your love and mercy, accept our adoration, praise, and thanksgiving.**

You have kept Your covenant, O Lord, with Your chosen people. **But we, Your chosen people in Christ, have often broken Your covenant.** In spite of our good intentions we have not always turned away from wickedness. **We have often questioned Your justice while remaining unjust ourselves.** Selfishness and conceit have often kept us from being of the same mind. **We lack the humility You require in our dealings with others.** We have elevated ourselves by being inconsiderate of the needs of our neighbor. **We have not adequately shown our appreciation for the sacrifice of Your Son Jesus Christ.** We have made promises to serve You and failed to keep our promises. **For these our countless transgressions, forgive us, Lord.**

Empower us by Your Holy Spirit to show true love and empathy. **Give us the spirit of Christ, who humbled Himself and became obedient unto death for our sakes.** Give us the will and the discipline to fulfill our promises. **Help us to be concerned about the affairs of others.** Protect our nation from enemies within and without.

(*Here special intercessions, silent or spoken, may be made. If spoken, each portion concludes:* Lord, in Your mercy, **hear our prayer.**)

In the name of Him who suffered, died, and rose again for our salvation, **Jesus Christ, our Lord, we pray. Amen**

TWENTIETH SUNDAY AFTER PENTECOST

Lord of the universe, Creator of heaven and earth, Redeemer of mankind, and Source of all power. **We, Your humble servants, come before You in the name of Jesus Christ, Your Son, our Savior.** Accept our praise and adoration for our creation, redemption, and sanctification.

You have transplanted us from the wilderness of this world into the vineyard of Your heavenly kingdom. As branches of that Great Vine, Jesus Christ, we have failed to produce the fruit You desire. **Instead of honor, we have often brought dishonor to Your name.** Our speech has often exceeded the bounds of truth, and we have not been sufficiently concerned that everyone be treated with justice. **We have entertained impure thoughts and glorified that which is unlovely.** We have been satisfied with mediocrity instead of striving for excellence.

May Your Holy Spirit, O Lord, give us the power to accomplish Your purposes. Grant peace to the nations of the earth and suppress all rebellion and anarchy. **Protect the innocent, provide food for the hungry, and give shelter to the homeless.** Give us Your Spirit of generosity to share our abundance with the needy. **Make us fruitful branches in Your vineyard, and help us to produce fruit with joy.** Especially, O Lord, help us to prepare the way for many to receive Your Son Jesus Christ as Lord of their lives and Savior of their souls.

(*Here special intercessions, silent or spoken, may be made. If spoken, each portion concludes:* Lord, in Your mercy, **hear our prayer.**)

Be with the sick, the lonely, and the discouraged. **We pray in the name of Jesus Christ, Your Son, our Savior. Amen**

TWENTY-FIRST SUNDAY AFTER PENTECOST

O Lord God, Shepherd of our souls and Supplier of all our needs, we, the people of Your pasture, come before You with hearts filled with gratitude and praise. **For leading us into the green pastures of Your Word, we give You thanks.** For leading us beside the still waters of Your love and mercy, we are most grateful. **For restoring our souls with the righteousness of Your Son Jesus Christ, we bring You our praise.** For making it possible for us to walk through the valley of the shadow of death without fear, we adore Your most holy name.

As Your sheep, O Lord, we acknowledge that we have often strayed from Your paths of righteousness. In the midst of abundance we have often been discontented. **In spite of Your loving care throughout our lives, we have often been anxious;** we doubted that You would supply all our needs. **For these, our many transgressions, forgive us, O Lord.**

Grant us Your Spirit and make us content with what You provide. **Give us the faith to realize that we can do all things through Christ, who strengthens us.** Be a source of strength to the Church, and bless our nation with peace. **Bring comfort to the sorrowing, and give hope to the discouraged.**

(*Here special intercessions, silent or spoken, may be made. If spoken, each portion concludes:* Lord, in Your mercy, **hear our prayer.**)

In the name of our Shepherd, Jesus Christ, **we bring these petitions before You. Amen**

TWENTY-SECOND SUNDAY AFTER PENTECOST

Almighty Creator and everlasting Redeemer, we ask You to look upon Your children whom You have called by Your name. **Daily we enjoy the gifts You provide.** Your heavenly dew falls on the just and the unjust. **Your sun shines on the evil and on the good.** Your mighty acts demonstrate that You are the true God. **We praise and thank You for exerting Your power for our benefit.** Especially are we grateful for sending us Your Son, our Savior, Jesus Christ.

Yet for all Your mercies, O Lord, we have fallen short of Your expectations. The light, which You brought into being by the power of Your Word, we have taken too much for granted. **The darkness, which You created, we have often used as a cover for our evil deeds.** We have neglected to give You adequate thanks for the works of faith of those who are called by Your name. **We have enjoyed good government, but we complain about paying our taxes to support it.** We have often neglected to render to You the things that are rightfully Yours. **Forgive us, O Lord.**

Enliven us with Your Holy Spirit, O Lord, that we may fulfill our calling. **Grant peace and unity to Your Church on earth that it may reflect Your honor and glory.** Inspire us to search Your Word for answers to our problems. **Keep us from expressing premature judgments against others.**

(*Here special intercessions, silent or spoken, may be made. If spoken, each portion concludes:* Lord, in Your mercy, **hear our prayer.**)

Bless our nation with peace, and help us dwell in harmony with Your will. **We pray in Jesus' name. Amen**

TWENTY-THIRD SUNDAY AFTER PENTECOST

O holy and righteous Lord, whose judgments are always right and just, we come before You, trusting that You will hear us. **Accept our praise and thanks for Your kindness and undeserved love.** For the light of another day and the protection of the past night, we give You thanks. **For making it possible for those who delight in Your law and Gospel to assemble before You, we are thankful.**

We readily confess that we have failed to measure up to the demands of Your law. **We have walked in the counsel of the wicked, stood in the way of sinners, and sat in the seat of the scornful.** We are far from being holy; we have been unjust in our judgments. **We have slandered our neighbor, borne grudges against him, and sought to pay back evil for evil.** We have not loved others as ourselves because we have not loved You with all our heart, with all our soul, and with all our mind. **For these departures from the demands of Your law, forgive us, O Lord.**

By Your Holy Spirit enable us to love You more fully by loving others. **Help us to love You as You have loved us.** May we be fruitful trees planted by the streams of Your Word. **Help us to meditate in Your Word day and night.** Give us joy in serving You, the only true God, and Jesus Christ, whom You have sent.

(*Here special intercessions, silent or spoken, may be made. If spoken, each portion concludes:* Lord, in Your mercy, **hear our prayer.**)

Grant us peace in our nation and in the world. **May Your Church reflect the love and harmony of our Lord Jesus Christ, in whose name we pray. Amen**

TWENTY-FOURTH SUNDAY AFTER PENTECOST

O Lord our God, our souls continually look for You. **We are restless until our souls are assured of Your presence.** We come to Your house of worship to consider Your mighty works and ponder Your glory. **Yours is the kingdom, the power, and the glory.** For the assurance of Your presence, we give You thanks.

We confess, O Lord, that we are not worthy of Your consideration, for we have often transgressed Your holy laws. We know from Your Word that the day of Your appearance and judgment is fast approaching; yet, we often live as if that day will never come. **In spite of Your assurance that those who are in Christ have nothing to fear, we become anxious when we contemplate the power You will reveal on that great day.** We have often depended upon the faith of others to prepare us to meet You. **Forgive us, for Jesus' sake.**

Keep alive the flame of faith within us by sending us Your Holy Spirit. **Guard us from believing that we can earn Your favor by our works.** Help us to believe that the righteousness of Jesus Christ is sufficient to cover all our sins.

Until the great day of Your visible return to earth, grant that we may live in peace and harmony with everyone. Curb the pride and greed of nations who want to subjugate the whole world to their way of thinking.

(Here special intercessions, silent or spoken, may be made. If spoken, each portion concludes: Lord, in Your mercy, **hear our prayer.**)

Protect our freedoms with Your great might, and keep us alert to subversive tendencies in our midst. **This we ask in the name of Jesus Christ, our Lord. Amen**

TWENTY-FIFTH SUNDAY AFTER PENTECOST

Every morning, O Lord, we experience the evidence of Your steadfast love. **We do not know, we cannot tell, what evils You have kept from us during the night.** In the confidence that whether we sleep or wake, we are Yours, O Lord, You have granted us refreshing rest. **For these Your many mercies, accept our thanks, O Lord.**

We confess that we have not always been dutiful servants. **Although You have given all of us talents, we have not always used them to the best interest of Your kingdom.** We have often failed to accept the challenge to put our talents to use in Your service. **We have hid them or used them to serve only ourselves.** We have neglected opportunities to develop them so that we might be of greater service to You and others. **For our negligence, forgive us, O Lord.**

May Your Holy Spirit inspire us to more dutiful service. **Help us to recognize the gifts that come from Your gracious hands.** Grant that the elected officials in church and state might use their talents for the good of all. **Help us to walk as children of the day.** Give us courage to express our hope of salvation in Christ Jesus. **Comfort the bereaved with hope in the resurrection.**

(*Here special intercessions, silent or spoken, may be made. If spoken, each portion concludes:* Lord, in Your mercy, **hear our prayer.**)

Give Your strength to the weak, courage to the disillusioned, and an awareness of Your presence to the lonely. **This we ask in the name of Jesus Christ, our Savior. Amen**

THIRD-LAST SUNDAY IN THE CHURCH YEAR

Eternal God and Father of all, accept our praises. **For generation after generation You have shown forth Your almighty power.** A thousand years in Your sight are like yesterday, and a day to You is like a thousand years to us. **In comparison, our lives are less than a day.** You satisfy us in the morning with Your steadfast love that we may rejoice and be glad all our days.

We come forth like a flower, wither, and fade like a shadow. From our birth we are full of sin; there is nothing in us that should attract Your love. **You determine the length of our days; we are powerless to extend Your limits.** In the short time allotted to us, help us, O Lord, to live our lives to Your honor and glory. **Help us to increase in love toward You, toward one another, and toward all people.** Send Your Holy Spirit to establish our hearts unblamable in the holiness of Jesus Christ, our Savior.

Then we shall have no fear on the day of Christ's coming, even if He comes like a flash of lightning. Give us faith and courage to endure any tribulation that may suddenly come upon us. **Above all, let us never be deceived by anyone pretending to be the Christ.** Enlighten our understanding that we may clearly identify our Savior and proclaim Him to others.

(*Here special intercessions, silent or spoken, may be made. If spoken, each portion concludes:* Lord, in Your mercy, **hear our prayer.**)

Grant peace to the nations of the world. **May Your Church have free course so that it can spread the Good News to the ends of the earth. This we ask in Jesus' name. Amen**

THIRD-LAST SUNDAY IN THE CHURCH YEAR (Alternate)

Lord God, heavenly Father, our help in ages past and our hope for years to come, we bring You our adoration, praise, and thanksgiving. **For keeping Your covenant with our forefathers and blessing us with the knowledge of forgiveness in Christ, we give You thanks.** Your mercies have been fresh every morning and Your kindness every night has not failed us.

All these blessings You have showered upon us, even though we have broken Your covenant. You desire the dedication of our whole heart, and yet we have served you halfheartedly. **You have warned us against hypocrisy, yet we have often been hypocritical.** Our actions have not always validated our words. **We tell others how they ought to live but fail to show them how.** We have exalted ourselves when we should have remained humble. **Spare us, O Lord, and restrain Your righteous anger because of our iniquities.** For the sake of the righteousness of Your Son, Jesus Christ, whom we claim as Savior, blot out our transgressions.

May Your Holy Spirit help us to live in conformity with the expression of our lips. Inspire us and give us the strength to live our religion from the heart. **Give genuineness of faith to our leaders in church and state.** Give peace to our souls and quietness to our minds.

(*Here special intercessions, silent or spoken, may be made. If spoken, each portion concludes:* Lord, in Your mercy, **hear our prayer.**)

May we serve You and others with love, sincerity, and truth. **Hear our prayer in the name of Jesus Christ. Amen**

SECOND-LAST SUNDAY IN THE CHURCH YEAR

We give thanks to You, O Lord, and call upon Your name. **We sing Your praises as we tell of Your wonderful works.** We seek Your strength and desire Your presence continually. **We remember the wonderful works You have done and the judgments You have uttered.** Again and again You have demonstrated in the world's history that nations who forget You and act contrary to Your will fall under Your judgment.

We confess, O Lord, that our nation is not without guilt. If You were to deal with us in justice, **we too would fall under Your judgment.** Therefore we do not ask that You deal with us justly, but we appeal to Your mercy. **For the sake of Your Son and our Savior Jesus Christ, we ask You to blot out our transgressions and remember our sins no more.**

You have not revealed the day and the hour when Christ will come again to judge the world. **Keep us steadfast in the faith by Your Spirit.** Give us zeal to proclaim the Gospel of Your kingdom throughout the world as a testimony to all nations. **May we be among those who will endure unto the end and thus be saved.**

Extend Your healing hand to the sick, Your presence to the lonely, Your hope to the discouraged, and Your comfort to the bereaved.

(*Here special intercessions, silent or spoken, may be made. If spoken, each portion concludes:* Lord, in Your mercy, **hear our prayer.**)

May Your peace permeate the councils of nations. **Grant harmony to Your Church on earth that Your will may be accomplished. In Jesus' name we pray. Amen**

SECOND-LAST SUNDAY IN THE CHURCH YEAR
(Alternate)

We give thanks to You, O Lord, and praise Your holy name. **Your name is well known throughout all the earth because of Your wonderful works.** We rejoice in Your presence as You strengthen our hearts. **Glory, honor, and thanks to you, O Lord our God, for Your gracious love in Jesus Christ, our Savior.**

You have set Your law before us, but we have not always walked according to it. **We have often failed to listen to Your Word from the mouth of Your servants.** For our apathy, indifference, and lack of zeal in doing Your will, forgive us, O Lord.

Grant us the strength of Your Holy Spirit to endure distress and affliction. Help us to stand firm and rejoice in the fellowship of other Christians. **Help us increase and abound in love toward one another.** Give us insight and understanding to recognize those who would deceive us with false teaching. **Give us the spiritual endurance to withstand the trials and tribulations that may come upon the earth in the last times.** Help us not to be alarmed or disturbed by wars and rumors of war, and give us the strength to endure persecutions because of our faith. **Help us to endure unto the end.** Give us a firm determination to spread Your Gospel throughout the whole world as a testimony to all nations. **May we continue to exercise our faith in the religious freedom of our country.**

(*Here special intercessions, silent or spoken, may be made. If spoken, each portion concludes:* Lord, in Your mercy, **hear our prayer.**)

Use us to bring Your Word of hope to the sick, the emotionally distressed, and the insecure. **This we ask in the name of our Lord and Savior Jesus Christ. Amen**

LAST SUNDAY IN THE CHURCH YEAR
Sunday of the Fulfillment

We serve You, O Lord, with gladness and come into Your presence with singing. **You have made us Your people and the sheep of Your pasture.** We enter Your gates with thanksgiving and Your courts with praise. **We give thanks to You for You are good and Your love endures forever.** Your faithfulness endures to all generations.

Your promise of creating new heavens and a new earth keeps us hopeful for the future. We shall then rejoice and be glad forever, for we shall hear no sound of weeping or cry of distress. **There will be no more death, and time will stand still.** Before we call, You will answer, and while we are yet speaking, You will hear. **We look forward to the indescribable peace that You have prepared for those who love You.**

Send us Your Holy Spirit that He may keep us alert and prepared to meet Christ, who will come as a bridegroom to claim His bride, the Church. **Help us keep our lamps filled with the oil of faith.** Protect us from the evil one, who would have us believe that we can enter the nuptial hall on the faith of someone else.

Keep us from thinking that Judgment Day will not come during our lifetime. Even though the earth be burned up and the elements melt with fervent heat, we will not fear. **According to Your promise in Christ Jesus assure us that we shall be with You in everlasting life.**

(*Here special intercessions, silent or spoken, may be made. If spoken, each portion concludes:* Lord, in Your mercy, **hear our prayer.**)

To enable us to spread Your kingdom without hindrance, **grant peace to our nation and the nations of the world. In Jesus' name we pray. Amen**

LAST SUNDAY IN THE CHURCH YEAR
Sunday of the Fulfillment (Alternate)

Almighty, everlasting God, Yours is the kingdom, the power, and the glory. **Accept our thanks for Your loving care of all people.** Especially do we thank You for choosing us to be in Your kingdom. **You have returned us, who were straying, lost, weak, and aimless, to Your fold.** For Your great mercy extended to us through Christ, Your Son, we give You thanks.

It is Your will that we show care and concern for one another, and yet we have often failed to carry out Your will. We have not been sufficiently concerned about feeding the hungry, welcoming strangers, or clothing the naked. **We have not visited the sick as often as we might, and we have often forgotten those who are in prison.** We so often forget that in serving our neighbor we are serving You. **For our thoughtlessness and failure to show our care and concern, forgive us, O Lord.**

May Your Holy Spirit guide us into the paths of concern and service. **Give us the spirit of sacrifice that we may be more willing and able to meet the needs of others.** Help us to remember that our deeds of charity do not earn us Your favor but reflect faith and gratitude for Your mercies. **Keep us alert and prepared for the day when Jesus will come as King to judge all nations.**

(*Here special intercessions, silent or spoken, may be made. If spoken, each portion concludes:* Lord, in Your mercy, **hear our prayer.**)

Preserve among us that form of government which makes it possible for us to show deeds of love toward one another. **Accept these petitions in the name of and for the sake of Jesus Christ, our King. Amen**

PRAYERS FOR SUNDAYS AND MAJOR FESTIVALS

Series B

FIRST SUNDAY IN ADVENT

O Lord, our Father and Redeemer, from everlasting You are God. **With joy and thanksgiving we acknowledge that we are indebted to You for our existence.** Without You we cannot live, and apart from You life has no meaning. **Bend down Your ear and listen as we pray.**

For permitting us to enter another church year, **we give You thanks.** For finding us and leading us like a shepherd through Your Word, **accept our heartfelt praise.** For keeping Your promise and sending us a Savior, **we praise Your holy name.**

In spite of Your loving-kindness, O Lord, we have often strayed from Your paths like lost sheep. **You love righteousness and hate wickedness, yet we have no righteousness of our own to offer You.** We all fade as the leaves, and because of our sin we are in constant danger of being blown away from Your presence. **For the many times we have caused You displeasure, we ask Your forgiveness.**

As we begin another year in Your kingdom of grace, send us Your Holy Spirit. **May the welcome of Your Son Jesus Christ into our hearts continue throughout the year.** Help us to acknowledge Him as Lord of our life not only for today, but for always. **Grant that in Him we may be enriched in our speech and knowledge.** Keep us watchful and alert that we may be ready to meet Him on that last great day.

(*Here special intercessions, silent or spoken, may be made. If spoken, each portion concludes:* Lord, in Your mercy, **hear our prayer.**)

As we prepare for the festivities of celebrating our Lord's birth, **grant us true spiritual insight that we may recognize Him as David's Son and David's Lord. Amen**

SECOND SUNDAY IN ADVENT

O Lord God, heavenly Father, as Your unworthy servants we come before You. **We give You hearty thanks for the comfort we receive from Your Word.** We are grateful for Your words of prophecy regarding the advent of Your Son Jesus Christ. **For the special messengers announcing His coming, we give You thanks.**

We confess, O Lord, that we are not worthy of such special attention. **The mountains of our sin should rightfully hide Your face from us.** Our lives have been as unproductive of good fruit as the desert. **Our failure to walk in the straight paths of Your commandments has nearly brought us into the valley of despair.** We have been less than zealous in living our lives in holiness and godliness. **We have often forgotten about Your coming to judge the whole earth.** We have sought forgiveness without genuine repentance. **For these and many other sins, we ask Your divine forgiveness.**

Help us, O Lord, to heed the cry of Your special messengers Isaiah and John the Baptist. **May Your Holy Spirit move us to genuine repentance that we may experience the comfort foretold by Your prophet Isaiah.** As the return of our Lord becomes more imminent, keep us alert and prepared to meet Him.

(*Here special intercessions, silent or spoken, may be made. If spoken, each portion concludes:* Lord, in Your mercy, **hear our prayer.**)

Since You are not willing that any should perish, bless our world with peace so that Your saving message will not be hindered. **May our own nation and its leaders work in harmony with Your will. In Jesus' name we pray. Amen**

THIRD SUNDAY IN ADVENT

We praise You, O God; we acknowledge You to be the Lord. **Heaven is Your throne and earth Your footstool.** From the beginning of creation to the present, You have shown Your concern for the welfare of the human race. **In times of trouble You have rescued us; in times of joy You have increased our happiness.** For Your steadfast love, O Lord, accept our heartfelt thanks.

We confess that we have not always rejoiced in our salvation. We have failed to give You thanks under all circumstances. **We have not always followed the promptings of Your Holy Spirit.** We have failed to hold on to all that is good, and we have not consistently abstained from every form of evil. **We have neglected to bear witness to the Light, Your Son Jesus Christ.** We often forget that Your will is being done through us in unpleasant as well as pleasant circumstances.

For our lack of zeal in acknowledging Your will for us, forgive us, O Lord. Help us not to quench the Holy Spirit within us. **Give us a clear understanding of our responsibilities.** As we have received from You the gift of salvation through our Lord Jesus Christ, may we reflect His light to all around us. **Strengthen our sense of good judgment that we may hold fast to what is good and abstain from every evil.** Use us to bring the good tidings to the afflicted, and help us bind up the brokenhearted.

(*Here special intercessions, silent or spoken, may be made. If spoken, each portion concludes:* Lord, in Your mercy, **hear our prayer.**)

Hasten the day of universal peace promised at Your Second Coming. **We ask it in Jesus' name. Amen**

FOURTH SUNDAY IN ADVENT

We will sing of Your steadfast love, O Lord, heavenly Father. **With our mouths we will proclaim Your faithfulness to all generations.** As we near the celebration of the birth of Your Son Jesus Christ, **we stand in awesome wonder of Your mysterious power and unapproachable wisdom.** For revealing to us Your plans for our salvation, conceived in the womb of eternity, announced by Your prophets, and brought forth in the fullness of time, **we praise and glorify Your most holy name.**

Only by faith in You as the only wise God can we recognize the great miracle that You performed in Your handmaiden, the Virgin Mary. **What You have done is above all human understanding.** When our reason doubts that Your love and mercy could accomplish this, **forgive us, O Lord.** For becoming impatient as You drive us to Your Word to search out Your prophecies regarding the unfolding of Your plan, **we ask Your forgiveness.**

As You sent Your Holy Spirit to inspire the prophets and the evangelists to speak and write Your Word, **so send Your Holy Spirit to us that we may truly believe Your truth.** May Your Spirit help us to believe what our reason cannot comprehend. **Fill our hearts with such joy that others may recognize these gifts as coming from You through our Lord Jesus Christ.**

(*Here special intercessions, silent or spoken, may be made. If spoken, each portion concludes:* Lord, in Your mercy, **hear our prayer.**)

We pray in the name of Your most precious gift, **Jesus Christ, our Lord and Savior. Amen**

THE NATIVITY OF OUR LORD

Praise, honor, and glory to You, O Lord our God. **With angels and archangels we magnify Your name: "Glory to God in the highest, and on earth peace among men with whom He is pleased."** We adore Your divine goodness and praise You for sending deliverance to Zion and for including us in the fulfillment of Your promises.

Even though we have no merit or worthiness within us, You have once again this Christmas assured us of Your love. Instead of justly punishing us, You have sent us salvation in the birth of Your Son. **In spite of our many transgressions You have made salvation possible in this gift of mercy.**

For rejoicing more in earthbound gifts than in Your heaven-sent gift, forgive us, O Lord. **For telling others more about earthly treasures than about the heavenly Word made flesh, forgive us, O Lord.** Accept our thanks for the eternal gift conceived out of Your love for the world. **Accept our thanks, O Lord, for bringing the knowledge of this divine truth to us.**

Bless, O Lord, the musicians, singers, and messengers who help us rejoice in Your Son's birth. **Bless the reception of this Good News in the hearts of those who hear it.** Bless, O Lord, the spread of the Christmas message throughout the world. **May these glad tidings bring hope to the discouraged and peace to the troubled.** May the lonely see in the Christmas message the assurance of Your presence.

(*Here special intercessions, silent or spoken, may be made. If spoken, each portion concludes:* Lord, in Your mercy, **hear our prayer.**)

May the peace of Christmas fill our nation and the nations of the world. **This we ask in the name of our Savior, Christ, the Lord. Amen**

FIRST SUNDAY AFTER CHRISTMAS

We give thanks to You, O Lord, for having sent redemption to Your people. **We praise You for keeping Your covenant established with our forefathers and proclaimed by Your prophets.** We give thanks to You with our whole heart and praise You for sending us salvation in the Babe of Bethlehem. **In spirit we kneel before His manger-throne, for in it You have revealed Your honor and majesty.**

We confess, O Lord, that our thankfulness for Your great salvation leaves much to be desired. **We have knelt at the manger, yet we have failed to let His Word dwell in us richly.** Compassion, kindness, lowliness, meekness, and patience have not always permeated our spirit. **We have experienced the joy of Your forgiveness but have often failed to forgive others.** The peace of Christ does not always rule our hearts, and we have not done everything in His name. **We often treat those within our family without demonstration of His love.** For failing to show adequate Christian concern, **O Lord, forgive us.**

Increase our faith by Your Holy Spirit that our Lord Jesus Christ may be for us a stepping-stone rather than a rock of offense. **Grant us strength and courage to acknowledge Him as our Lord and Savior.**

(*Here special intercessions, silent or spoken, may be made. If spoken, each portion concludes:* Lord, in Your mercy, **hear our prayer.**)

Bless our witness that it may bring others to the Light of their salvation. **This we ask in the name of and for the sake of our Lord and Savior Jesus Christ. Amen**

SECOND SUNDAY AFTER CHRISTMAS

O God and Father of our Lord Jesus Christ, who has blessed us with every spiritual blessing in Christ, **we praise and adore You for choosing us in Him before the foundation of the world.** We cannot understand how this is possible, but we believe it because of the clear testimony of Your Word. **You destined us in love to be Your children through Christ, according to the purpose of Your will.**

You have chosen us, O Lord, that we should be holy and blameless before You. **Because of the weakness of our flesh, however, we are unable to achieve Your purpose.** But thanks be to You, for through Your Son Jesus Christ You have made us holy and blameless. **He took upon Himself our flesh and dwelt among us.** He has revealed Your glory as a light shining in the darkness. **From His fullness of glory we have received Your grace.** Now we know that we can stand before You in His righteousness. **For this, Your grace and mercy, accept our humble thanks.**

As You sent John the Baptist to point to the Light, which shines in the darkness, so also empower us with Your Spirit to bear witness to that Light. **You have given us power to receive Him, to believe in His name, and thereby to become Your children.** For the grace and truth we have received through Him, **we give You humble thanks.**

(*Here special intercessions, silent or spoken, may be made. If spoken, each portion concludes:* Lord, in Your mercy, **hear our prayer.**)

In the name of Him whose light still shines to all the world for the salvation of many, **we pray. Amen**

THE EPIPHANY OF OUR LORD

Dear heavenly Father, in the darkness of this world's spiritual night, You created a special star to guide the Wise Men to Your Son. **For this revelation of Your glory, we give You humble thanks.** For predicting this event through your prophet Isaiah, hundreds of years before it took place, **We praise and adore You.**

Like Herod, we have often been guilty of being insincere in our search for Christ. **Forgive us, O Lord.** We have often failed to show others the way to Him, who is the Truth and the Light. **Have mercy on us, O Lord.** We confess that we have not always permitted Your Son to be the Light of our life. **Forgive us, O Lord.**

For guiding Gentiles to the birthplace of Your Son Jesus and for accepting their worship as fellow heirs and partakers of the promise in Christ Jesus through the Gospel, **we give You thanks.** For making it possible for us to become Your children through Christ, **we are eternally grateful.**

Send us Your Holy Spirit that He may increase our understanding of the magnitude of Your love. **Loosen our tongues and give us courage to tell the Good News to a world still largely in darkness.** Motivate us to generosity in bringing our gifts for the extension of Your kingdom. **Extend Your healing hand to the sick and Your presence to the lonely.**

(*Here special intercessions, silent or spoken, may be made. If spoken, each portion concludes:* Lord, in Your mercy, **hear our prayer.**)

Grant our government and the governments of the world sincere, honest, and wise officials. **We bring these our petitions in the name of Jesus Christ, our Lord and Savior. Amen**

THE BAPTISM OF OUR LORD
First Sunday after the Epiphany

Almighty and gracious God, Creator and Judge of all people, Father of our Lord Jesus Christ, **we praise You for Your concern to establish justice on the earth.** We thank You for sending Your Servant, our Lord Jesus Christ, to bring justice to all nations. **We thank You for identifying Him as Your beloved Son by anointing Him with the Holy Spirit and power at His baptism.** For revealing Yourself as the Triune God at the baptism of our Lord, we give You humble and hearty thanks. **Now we know for certain that He is Your Son whom You sent to redeem us from sin, death, and the power of Satan.**

We confess, O Lord, that we have no righteousness of our own. **We are truly thankful that in our baptism You have given us forgiveness, life, and salvation.** For forgetting the significance of our baptism, **forgive us, O Lord.** For not measuring up to our high calling as Your sons and daughters, **we ask Your forgiveness.** We do not appeal to Your justice to deal with us as we deserve, but we appeal to Your mercy. **Have mercy on us, O Lord.**

As You anointed Your Son with the Holy Spirit and power, **help us to remember that through our baptism the Holy Spirit has given us the power to accept the baptized Christ as our Savior.**

(*Here special intercessions, silent or spoken, may be made. If spoken, each portion concludes:* Lord, in Your mercy, **hear our prayer.**)

Help us to establish and maintain justice on earth, that all nations may hear the Good News that in Jesus Christ there is peace. **This we ask in the name of Jesus. Amen**

SECOND SUNDAY AFTER THE EPIPHANY

Lord God, heavenly Father, You have been gracious to us and blessed us. **The earth has yielded its increase, and Your way is being made known to many nations.** For bringing the knowledge of salvation to our nation and increasingly to other nations, **we adore Your most holy name.**

We confess, O Lord, that we have too often taken Your blessings for granted. **We have neglected our primary mission to proclaim Your way within our own nation and to other nations.** Although You have revealed Yourself to us in Your Word, we have often ignored Your voice calling us to action. **We have not always respected our bodies as temples of the Holy Spirit.** We have been hesitant to admonish others who abuse their bodies. **We have done too little to stem the tide of immorality in our nation.** For our many sins of neglect, **forgive us, O Lord.**

Give us the courage and the strength to be more faithful in inviting others to follow You. **May Your Holy Spirit motivate us actively to share Christ with others by our words and deeds.** Bless our national and world leaders that they may lead in a way which is acceptable in Your sight. **May all people know Your love in Christ.** Comfort the bereaved with the blessed hope of the resurrection in Christ.

(*Here special intercessions, silent or spoken, may be made. If spoken, each portion concludes:* Lord, in Your mercy, **hear our prayer.**)

Give strength to the weak and companionship to the lonely. **This we ask in the name of Jesus Christ, Your Son and our Savior. Amen**

THIRD SUNDAY AFTER THE EPIPHANY

Steadfast love, O Lord, is Yours forever. **You have shown us Your love every day of our lives.** We have seen it in the daily rising of the sun and in the moon and stars, which keep in their appointed courses. **Your love drops down on us in the snow and in the rain, giving seed to the sower and bread to the eater.** But we praise You most of all for being the Rock of our salvation. **In love Your mighty power has brought us the salvation of our souls in Your Son Jesus Christ.** For all these mercies, **accept our heartfelt thanks.**

We confess, O Lord, that we have returned disobedience for Your love. **Our cities need Your prophets as much as Nineveh did.** We are ashamed, O Lord, of our failure to preach repentance. **We have often behaved as children of the world rather than as Your children.** We know You want us to be fishers of men, and still we are reluctant to accomplish Your mission. **We follow You too often at a distance, hesitant to get involved in Your kingdom.** For our lack of zeal in calling the world to repentance and proclaiming the Gospel, **forgive us, O Lord.**

Give us strength to overcome the weakness of our flesh. **Give us the courage to stand up for what is right in Your sight.** Help us to repent and believe the Gospel. **Confirm our faith in Your Word and sacraments.** Bless our government with peace, harmony, and wisdom. **May those who are afflicted see in Jesus the source for hope and healing.**

(*Here special intercessions, silent or spoken, may be made. If spoken, each portion concludes:* Lord, in Your mercy, **hear our prayer.**)

Give ear, O Lord, to our prayers and heed the voice of our supplications. **In Jesus' name we pray. Amen**

FOURTH SUNDAY AFTER THE EPIPHANY

We thank You, our heavenly Father, for the care you have extended to us during the night. **We praise You for permitting us to see the light of another day.** Glorious are all Your works and marvelous are all Your words. **For putting Your Word in the mouth of Your prophets, we praise and glorify You.** For raising up a prophet like Yourself from our midst, even our own Lord Jesus Christ, we adore Your most holy name. **For the full revelation of Your will in Your Word made flesh, we praise You.**

We confess, O Lord, that in spite of the clear revelation of Your will through Your Word, we have often failed to carry out Your will. **We have walked in the counsel of the wicked and have stood in the way of sinners.** We have frequently been scornful. **We have not been sufficiently careful about our way of life and have thereby possibly offended the weak.** We have not meditated on Your Word day and night, nor have we produced fruit like a tree by the streams of water. **We have not always revealed Your full truth to others, nor have we been sufficiently careful to limit our conversation to Your truth.** For these, our many transgressions, **forgive us, O Lord.**

Send us Your Holy Spirit that we may live in conformity to Your holy will. **Strengthen our faith in the truth of Your Word, and help us live according to it.** Keep us considerate of the needs of others and safeguard our freedoms in this beloved land.

(*Here special intercessions, silent or spoken, may be made. If spoken, each portion concludes:* Lord, in Your mercy, **hear our prayer.**)

Grant peace to us and all people. **We pray in Jesus' name. Amen**

FIFTH SUNDAY AFTER THE EPIPHANY

Father in heaven, may Your kingdom come among us, your humble servants. **We thank You for the revelation of Jesus as Lord and Christ and as King forever.** We pray that His dominion may be established from the rising to the setting of the sun. **We praise You for sending us a King whose law is love, whose crown is truth, and whose scepter is righteousness.** We pray that one day every nation, kindred, and tribe may confess that Jesus is Lord.

May Your kingdom come to everyone on earth so that all rulers and subjects bow before Your Son Jesus Christ. **Let all the earth see that in Him alone can healing be found for its wounds.** Bare Your holy arm and make those who spread violence among us know that You are a God whose laws must be obeyed. **May Your law and Your justice prevail.** Bring to naught the plans of those who seek to achieve their goals by taking the law into their own hands. **Protect us from the violence of terrorists and others who would seek to do us harm.**

Because of our sins we have no right to expect Your divine consideration, **but we come to You in the righteousness of Jesus Christ, Your Son.** By His merit we ask Your forgiveness and Your mercy. **Give comfort to those who mourn and give patience to the sick.** Give strength to the weak and abundance to the needy.

(*Here special intercessions, silent or spoken, may be made. If spoken, each portion concludes:* Lord, in Your mercy, **hear our prayer.**)

Give forgiveness to the penitent and sanity to the rebellious. **We pray in the precious name of Jesus Christ, our Lord and Savior. Amen**

SIXTH SUNDAY AFTER THE EPIPHANY

Almighty and merciful God, we praise You for being more ready to forgive than to condemn. **Because You are willing to cover our sin with the blood of Your Son Jesus Christ, we come to You in His name.** Accept our praise and adoration for Your miracle of cleansing. **With the washing of the water by the Word, You have made us Your children, for which we give You thanks.**

Forgive us when we have doubted Your willingness to cleanse us from the leprosy of our sin. **By nature we are tempted to think we can cleanse ourselves with our own righteousness.** Preserve us from such self-deception, and send us Your Holy Spirit that we may be willing to accept Your way of cleansing. **Help us to show our thanks by avoiding what You forbid and doing what You command.** Give us the insight to understand that even our eating and drinking can be done to Your honor and glory. **Give us grace not to offend the weak.** Give us not only the desire but also the strength to be imitators of Your Son Jesus Christ.

Preserve the liberty and freedom for which our nation stands. Be a source of strength to the weak and joy to the sorrowful and depressed. **Grant companionship to the lonely and hope to the discouraged.** Above all, help us to show You our thanks for being cleansed through the blood of Your Son Jesus Christ.

(*Here special intercessions, silent or spoken, may be made. If spoken, each portion concludes:* Lord, in Your mercy, **hear our prayer.**)

Help us to share this Good News with others. **We ask this in the name of Jesus Christ, our Lord. Amen**

SEVENTH SUNDAY AFTER THE EPIPHANY

Lord God, heavenly Father, healer of our souls and caretaker of our bodies, **accept our praise for the spiritual and physical blessings You extend to us every day.** We have nothing to offer You but our sins, and yet You tell us that You will remember our sins no more. **For the peace of mind and quietness of soul this assurance gives us, accept our thanks.**

Without the gift of Your Son Jesus Christ we would still be in despair because of our sins, **and we would be unable to bear the burdens of physical afflictions.** You have changed our despair into hope by the assurance of Your salvation. **All Your promises are made certain in Jesus Christ, our Lord.**

Send us Your Holy Spirit that He may keep us firm in our faith. **Help us to recognize the real needs of others, and bless our efforts toward meeting those needs.** As Your Son Jesus Christ first met the spiritual needs of the paralytic, help us to be concerned about our neighbors' spiritual as well as physical needs. **As You once used Your power to relieve believers of their diseases, may that power still be evident among us.**

(*Here special intercessions, silent or spoken, may be made. If spoken, each portion concludes:* Lord, in Your mercy, **hear our prayer.**)

Bless our nation with peace, and help us to dwell in harmony with Your will. **Help Your Church fulfill its primary mission and assure us of Your presence. In Jesus' name we pray. Amen**

EIGHTH SUNDAY AFTER THE EPIPHANY

Blessed are You, O Lord, and blessed is Your holy name. **You forgive all our iniquities and heal our diseases.** You redeem us from destruction and crown us with steadfast love and mercy. **You renew our youth like the eagle's by satisfying us with good things.** You do not deal with us according to our sins, nor repay us according to our iniquities. **Accept, O Lord, our sacrifice of praise and thanksgiving.**

We confess that our lives have not always been letters of recommendation. **We have often been guilty of trying to keep the letter of the Law, while forgetting its spirit.** As letters of Christ to a world lost in religious confusion, our testimony leaves much to be desired. **We have often attempted to mend the flaws in our lives with patches of our own good works.** For our failure to live up to Your expectations, forgive us, O Lord.

Visit us with Your Holy Spirit, and change our hearts to love You more completely. Help us to rejoice in Your mercy as revealed to us by Your Son Jesus Christ. **Grant us serenity in the midst of trials and afflictions.** Give us power to be worthy examples of Your love in a loveless world. **Permeate the councils of nations and of our own nation with Your spirit of justice, mercy, and forgiveness.**

(Here special intercessions, silent or spoken, may be made. If spoken, each portion concludes: Lord, in Your mercy, **hear our prayer.**)

Extend Your healing hand to the sick, Your presence to the lonely, and Your hope of everlasting life to the bereaved. **We pray in Jesus' name. Amen**

THE TRANSFIGURATION OF OUR LORD
Last Sunday after the Epiphany

Almighty God, Lawgiver and Redeemer of the human race, we come before You in awe and wonder. **Your laws have saved humanity from anarchy and chaos; Your statutes help preserve our existence on this earth.** For preserving Your precepts through Moses, Elijah, and Your Son Jesus Christ, **we give You most hearty thanks.**

We confess that, although You have made Your will known through a succession of Your prophets down to the present day, we have not sufficiently treasured Your law and Gospel. **We have transgressed Your law and neglected many opportunities to spread Your Gospel.** We have been guilty of doubting the divine revelation of Your Word. **We have often given our own private interpretation before seeking the clear message of Your Word.** With itching ears we have listened for new doctrines, the commandments of men. **For our lack of careful concern to accurately determine Your will, forgive us, O Lord.**

Through Your beloved Son Jesus Christ You have revealed Your Word in the flesh. **Send us Your Holy Spirit that we may hear Him speaking to us in Your Word.** Give us the courage to hold high the light of Your Word to those who sit in darkness, **and bless it in the hearts of those who hear it.**

(Here special intercessions, silent or spoken, may be made. If spoken, each portion concludes: Lord, in Your mercy, **hear our prayer.***)*

We humbly thank You for permitting us to bask in the light of Your truth. **Lead us one day into the presence of Him who is this world's Light. In His most holy name we pray. Amen**

ASH WEDNESDAY

O God, Father of our Lord Jesus Christ and also our dear Father, **we thank You for permitting us to begin another Lenten season.** We are again privileged to meditate upon the cross of Christ and its meaning for us. **You have graciously granted us another opportunity for our relationship to be strengthened with Him who died to save us from our sins.** For Your gracious love, which prompted You to punish Your Son for our sins, **we give You humble and hearty thanks.**

In spirit we appear before You in sackcloth and ashes. **Send us Your Holy Spirit that He may help us to be genuinely sorry for our sins.** Help us to withstand the temptations of permitting the pleasures of this life, the worries of the day, and the activities of our daily routine to interfere with our Lenten worship and observance. **Draw us to Your wounded side and bring healing to our souls.** By Your grace help us to crucify our sinful desires, affections, and lusts. **Help us to be conquerors over every temptation that confronts us.**

(*Here special intercessions, silent or spoken, may be made. If spoken, each portion concludes:* Lord, in Your mercy, **hear our prayer.**)

Grant to Your Church an awareness of its responsibility to bring the Good News to everyone in the community. **Graciously bestow on us Your Holy Spirit so we may bear witness to You as our Savior.** To this end bless our Lenten services. **Grant us faithful attendance, and open our eyes to the opportunities for bringing others.** Add Your blessing to the Lenten messages, and through them strengthen our faith in Jesus Christ as our Savior. **This we ask in Jesus' name. Amen**

FIRST SUNDAY IN LENT

Gracious Lord, Father of Abraham, Isaac, and Jacob, we, Your chosen ones in Christ Jesus, bring to You our sacrifice of prayer and praise. **For not rebuking us in Your anger or chastening us in Your wrath, we give You thanks.** For hearing our supplications and accepting our prayers, **we adore Your most holy name.**

As Abraham passed the test when You challenged him to offer up his only son, **so grant us the strength of faith to be willing to sacrifice our most beloved possessions for the interests of Your kingdom.** As Your Son Jesus Christ withstood the temptations of Satan in the wilderness, grant us the power to overcome him in our daily lives. **As You sent Your angels to serve Jesus, may Your angels be with us when Satan challenges us to sin.** Yours is the kingdom, the power, and the glory. **May we always be ready for the unknown hour when You come to receive us into Your kingdom of glory.** Send us Your Holy Spirit that He may keep us steadfast in the Christian faith. **In every trial and temptation may nothing separate us from Your love in Christ Jesus.** Help us to be more than conquerors through Him who loved us.

(*Here special intercessions, silent or spoken, may be made. If spoken, each portion concludes:* Lord, in your mercy, **hear our prayer.**)

While we wait for the fulfillment of Your promises regarding Your kingdom, grant Your continual blessing to our nation and the nations of the earth. **Give us peace in our time that Your Gospel may have free course to the ends of the earth. In Jesus' name we pray. Amen**

SECOND SUNDAY IN LENT

We give glory to Your name, O Lord, for Your steadfast love and faithfulness. **Our trust in You has never been misplaced, for You have been our help and shield.** You have been mindful of Your own, and we have experienced Your blessings. **From this time forth and even forevermore we bless and praise You, O Lord.**

We regret, gracious Father, that we have often caused You sorrow by our many transgressions. **We have not rejoiced in our sufferings, nor have we denied ourselves in order to take up our cross and follow Your Son.** We have been reluctant to sacrifice any of our comforts for His sake. **We have neglected many opportunities to confess Him before others.** For our many sins of neglect we beg Your forgiveness.

Send us Your Holy Spirit that He may strengthen our faith in our Savior Jesus Christ. Help us to trust in Him as the only way between earth and heaven. **Lead us to recognize that through suffering for Your sake we develop endurance, which lets us live in hope.** May we constantly rejoice in the certainty of our salvation.

Guide the leaders of our nation and all nations in the way of Your truth. Give them the desire to fulfill their duties in accordance with Your will. **Give strength to the weak and hope to the discouraged.** May the lonely be assured of Your presence.

(*Here special intercessions, silent or spoken, may be made. If spoken, each portion concludes:* Lord, in Your mercy, **hear our prayer.**)

This we ask in the name of Him who justified us in Your sight by His blood, **even Jesus Christ, our Lord. Amen**

THIRD SUNDAY IN LENT

Let the words of our mouths and the meditations of our hearts be acceptable in Your sight, O Lord. **When we consider the perfection of Your laws, O Lord, we realize how far we have strayed from the way in which You would have us walk.**

We have all too frequently feared, loved, and trusted other things and other people more than You. **In moments of weakness we have taken Your name in vain.** We have not always put forth our best efforts to worship in Your house on Your day. **Our respect for the authority of those You have placed over us leaves much to be desired.** We have shortened the lives of others by hurting them in thought, word, and deed. **We have encouraged immorality by permitting the attitude of the world to lower our standards.** We have often failed to respect the property rights of others and have not always explained their mistakes in the best possible way. **In spite of our abundance we are guilty of grumbling and being discontented.**

For our transgressions we implore Your forgiveness in the name of Jesus Christ, our Savior. **Send us Your Holy Spirit that He may give us power to overcome our human frailties.** Help us to be better examples to the world in which we live.

(*Here special intercessions, silent or spoken, may be made. If spoken, each portion concludes:* Lord, in Your mercy, **hear our prayer.**)

May our nation carry out its responsibilities in the council of nations. **Bless the witness of Your Church that we may lead the world to know the goodness of Your law and accept the truth of Your Gospel. In Jesus' name we pray. Amen**

FOURTH SUNDAY IN LENT

Lord God, heavenly Father, You are the Light of our life and the Hope of our salvation. **With You as our God we have nothing to fear.** You protect us from our enemies and are the source of all our joy and happiness. **Accept the grateful melodies of our hearts, and listen to our songs of praise.**

Forgive us, O Lord, for the times we have murmured against You and have been discontented with our life. **In the midst of abundance we have often been critical of Your providence.** Walking through the wilderness of this world, we have often failed to look up to Him whom You raised for our salvation. **We have often looked elsewhere than to Your grace and mercy to find a cure for our ills.** Having a knowledge of Your truth, we have often permitted ourselves to be misled by the deceit and cunning of men. **For these and many other transgressions, forgive us, O Lord.**

Grant us power through Your Holy Spirit to trust in the merits of Jesus Christ, our Savior, rather than in our own attempted goodness. **Help us to accept Your love in Your only-begotten Son.** Enable us to hold high the banner of Your love in Christ that whoever believes in Him should not perish but have everlasting life. **Help us to lead the world out of darkness into Your marvelous light.**

Grant that our nation may increase in obedience to Your law and Gospel. **According to Your will, heal the sick, strengthen the faith of all doubters, and lift up the depressed.**

(*Here special intercessions, silent or spoken, may be made. If spoken, each portion concludes:* Lord, in Your mercy, **hear our prayer.**)

Break the solitude of the lonely with Your presence. **This we ask in the name of Jesus, our Savior. Amen**

FIFTH SUNDAY IN LENT

Open our lips, O Lord, and our mouths shall show forth Your praise. **Restore unto us the joy of our salvation, and uphold us with a willing spirit.** Put Your law within our hearts, and help us to be Your people. **Then we will teach transgressors Your ways, and sinners will return to You.**

We give You heartfelt thanks, O Lord, for sending Your Son Jesus Christ, who, being perfect, has become the Source of our salvation.

We acknowledge, O Lord, that we are undeserving of Your grace and mercy. Our love for the world has often made us reluctant to serve You. **We want to be with you, but hesitate to follow You.** We have not always honored You with our service. **For our lack of zeal and self-sacrifice, forgive us, O Lord.**

Send us Your Holy Spirit that we may properly glorify You and Your Son. **Give us the zeal that would help us show others a vision of Your glory.** Grant us wisdom and understanding to lead our nation and the nations of the earth to the foot of Christ's cross. **Give to Your Church a deep sense of dedication to its mission of proclaiming the death and resurrection of Your Son Jesus Christ.**

(*Here special intercessions, silent or spoken, may be made. If spoken, each portion concludes:* Lord, in Your mercy, **hear our prayer.**)

Give to the lonely an awareness of Your presence, to the sick, the hope of healing through Your power, and to the depressed, a goal for living. **This we ask in the name of Jesus Christ, Your Son and our Savior. Amen**

PALM SUNDAY
Sunday of the Passion

With hosannas we come before You, O Lord of hosts. **We praise You for sending Your Son as the King who came in Your name to establish peace between heaven and earth.** We are thankful that He did not consider Himself too far above us to humble Himself and come as true Man. **We deeply appreciate His fulfillment of the Law, which we are unable to keep.** Words fail us when we try to express our thanks that Christ took our punishment upon Himself by dying on the cross.

O Lord Jesus Christ, today we confess that we have not always been faithful to our calling as Your chosen people. The deeds of our lives often have not matched the confession of our lips. **We could have been more faithful in the use of Your Word and sacraments.** By neglecting prayer, we have often broken communication with You.

Because we know, O Lord, that you are merciful, we dare to come before You, asking forgiveness. May the assurance of that forgiveness, which we receive through Your Word and sacraments, help us be dedicated disciples.

Send us Your Holy Spirit to keep us on the path that leads to You. Enable us to withstand the temptations of Satan, the world, and our flesh. **Grant us grace to live to Your honor and glory,** so that our lives will reflect our eternal gratitude for the salvation You won for us through Your life of perfect obedience and through Your sacrificial suffering and death.

(*Here special intercessions, silent or spoken, may be made. If spoken, each portion concludes:* Lord, in Your mercy, **hear our prayer.**)

Bless our nation with peace, and help us dwell in harmony with Your will. **This we ask in the name of the King of kings and Lord of lords, Jesus Christ, our Savior. Amen**

MAUNDY THURSDAY

Lord God, heavenly Father, Author of the everlasting covenant and Giver of the cup of salvation, **we Your children gather in Your courts to offer to You our sacrifice of thanksgiving.** For fulfilling Your promise to establish a new covenant through the blood of Your Son Jesus Christ, **we give You humble and hearty thanks.** Through the veil of His flesh **we enter the Holy of Holies of Your presence without fear or trembling.** As our Lord Jesus Christ gave thanks to You when He broke the bread, **so we give You thanks.** As He gave You thanks when He took the cup, **so we give You thanks.**

Lord Jesus Christ, both our High Priest and the offering, **awe and wonder fill our hearts as we partake of Your body, broken for us, and Your blood, shed for us.** In our poverty of righteousness we have nothing to offer but our gratitude for Your perfect righteousness. **Were it not for Your tremendous sacrifice, we would still be in our sins.** But thanks be to You, for through Your Sacrament of the New Testament **we are assured that our iniquities are forgiven and our sins are no longer remembered.**

O Holy Spirit, dwell within us as we remember in this Sacrament our Lord's death. **Enter our hearts, and help us to show our gratitude by encouraging one another to love and good works.**

(*Here special intercessions, silent or spoken, may be made. If spoken, each portion concludes:* Lord, in Your mercy, **hear our prayer.**)

Help us to live our lives as sacrifices of thanksgiving **to Him who first loved us. May our love for Him express itself in love and service to one another. In His name we pray. Amen**

GOOD FRIDAY

Lord God, heavenly Father, this day marks the anniversary of Your greatest gift to the world. **Your love for the human race is beyond our understanding.** We praise You for that love, which caused You to give up Your only-begotten Son unto death for sinful humanity. **Cleansed of our sin and clothed in His righteousness, we can now stand in Your presence.** We thank You for making us the beneficiaries of Your love in Christ.

O Lord Jesus Christ, we will never know the full extent of Your suffering for us. Because You asked Your Father to forgive those who put You on the cross, we know that our sins have also been forgiven. **Because You promised the criminal who believed in You everlasting life,** we have the assurance that, in spite of our sins, we too may have eternal life. **As in the midst of Your suffering You had consideration for Your mother,** we can be confident You will be with us to the end of our earthly life. **Because You were forsaken by God the Father,** we know that we shall never be forsaken. **Because You thirsted for us,** we now have the water of everlasting life. **Because of Your declaration that the work of redemption was finished,** we no longer need to be doubtful about our salvation. **Through Your yielding up Your spirit to death,** we have life.

O Holy Spirit, abide in our hearts. Help us to believe that Christ died in our place. **Grant us a faith that bears testimony to our friends and community that this salvation is also available to them.**

(*Here special intercessions, silent or spoken, may be made. If spoken, each portion concludes:* Lord, in Your mercy, **hear our prayer.**)

So fill us with Your Holy Spirit that our lives will be a constant witness to our faith in the crucified Christ. **This we ask in the name of Jesus Christ, our Lord and Savior. Amen**

THE RESURRECTION OF OUR LORD
Easter Day

O God of life and Father of our Lord Jesus Christ, according to Your abundant grace, **You have begotten us again unto a new and living hope by the resurrection of Jesus from the dead.** You have transformed the night of doubt and sorrow into the new and eternal day of joy and gladness. **You have brought life and immortality to light by the glad tidings that Christ is risen. For this, O Lord, we give you thanks.** You have delivered from the grip of death Your Son, who died for our sins, and raised Him by Your power. **What You sowed in dishonor and weakness, You raised in power and glory.** O God, we praise You that through Him You removed for us death's sting. **You have brought us victory over the grave.**

Fill our hearts with the joy of the resurrection. **Grant to Your Church and people everywhere the power of an endless life.** Help us to show forth Your praises. **Bless our homes with Easter's comfort and hope.** Send the conquering banner of Christ's victory into all the world. **Grant that many more nations may join the hosts of heaven in songs of triumph.**

In the promise of Easter take away from us all fear of death. **Let the radiant beams of Easter's light shine into the depths of our souls.** Renew us in the Spirit of Him who is the way, the truth, and the life. **Speak peace to our souls, and maintain our faith in Him who promises resurrection and life.** Visit with Your presence those who are lonely.

(*Here special intercessions, silent or spoken, may be made. If spoken, each portion concludes:* Lord, in Your mercy, **hear our prayer.**)

Heal the sick and give courage to the discouraged. **This we ask in the name of our risen Lord. Amen**

SECOND SUNDAY OF EASTER

Lord God, heavenly Father, we praise Your most holy name. **Your name is exalted above earth and heaven.** We praise You for raising Your Son Jesus Christ from the dead. **You have opened to us the gates of eternal life.**

For failing to return Your love, **forgive us, O Lord.** For not obeying Your commandments, **we ask Your forgiveness.** For failing to overcome the temptations of the world, **forgive us, O Lord.** For so often being like Thomas and looking for visible proofs of Your presence, **we ask Your forgiveness.**

Send us Your Holy Spirit that we may believe without seeing. **Help us to accept the peace that comes from acknowledging Jesus Christ as Your Son.** Help us to share this peace with others by extending to them Your forgiveness. **As You sent Your Son to redeem us, so may we willingly go where He sends us.** May others see in us the joy which comes from knowing the resurrected Lord. **Make us agents of Your joy and peace in this world filled with sorrow and strife.** May our faith in Your Son give us the victory that overcomes the world.

Grant to the leaders of our nation wisdom and understanding that they may govern according to Your will. May Your Church show forth the joy and gladness that comes from a faith centered in our resurrected Lord. **Help us to be friends to the friendless and bearers of hope to the hopeless.**

(*Here special intercessions, silent or spoken, may be made. If spoken, each portion concludes:* Lord, in Your mercy, **hear our prayer.**)

Help us to be a source of strength to the weak and messengers of salvation to the straying and lost. **This we ask in the name of our resurrected Lord, Your Son, our Savior, Jesus Christ. Amen**

THIRD SUNDAY OF EASTER

You have searched us and known us, O Lord. **You know when we sit down and when we rise up.** You understand our thoughts from afar. **You search out our paths and our lying down.** You are acquainted with all our ways. **You know what words we are going to speak even before we utter them.** Such knowledge is too wonderful for us. **We adore Your most holy name.**

We are grateful for the accounts of witnesses who saw the resurrected Lord with their own eyes and touched Him with their own hands. **Because He rose from the dead, we can now have fellowship with You, with Him, and with one another.**

Most important of all, because of His resurrection, we know that when we confess our sins, we are assured of Your forgiveness. **This puts real meaning into our lives and gives us courage to face any difficulty that may lie ahead.**

O Lord Jesus Christ, as You opened the minds of Your first disciples to understand the Scriptures, **so open our minds that we may know Your will for us.** Send us the power of the Holy Spirit so that we may be able witnesses to Your resurrection. **In a world which seems so preoccupied with death, may we show where real life can be found.** Grant Your continued presence in our nation. **Help us to enlist all nations in Your cause.**

(*Here special intercessions, silent or spoken, may be made. If spoken, each portion concludes:* Lord, in Your mercy, **hear our prayer.**)

Clothe us with power from on high to help us proclaim the promises of our heavenly Father. **This we ask in Your most holy name. Amen**

FOURTH SUNDAY OF EASTER

Lord God, heavenly Father, Shepherd of our souls, we come before You as those who have been called into Your one flock. **We give you humble and hearty thanks that in Your mercy You have fed us in the green pastures of Your Word.** By giving us the knowledge of salvation through Jesus Christ Your Son, You have led us to the still waters that bring peace to our souls. **For Your loving and gracious care, which You lavish on us without any merit or worthiness in us, we give You thanks.**

We confess that we have often strayed like lost sheep seeking greener pastures. **Yet we know that You alone have the words of eternal life which satisfy our souls.** We have often left the paths of Your righteousness to walk in the ways of this world, seeking our own righteousness. **For forgetting that Your Son laid down His life for us so that we might walk in Your ways, forgive us, O Lord.**

Give us the gift of Your Holy Spirit in abundant measure that we may have strength to walk in the paths of Your righteousness. **Renew in us the determination to proclaim to the world that you desire everyone to come into Your fold.** May the power of Your Son Jesus, which enabled Your apostles to heal the sick and restore the crippled, still be manifested in our midst today. **Grant Your blessings to the leaders of our nation in church and state.**

(*Here special intercessions, silent or spoken, may be made. If spoken, each portion concludes:* Lord, in Your mercy, **hear our prayer.**)

Be with our leaders at all levels of government, heal the sick, and assure the lonely of Your presence. **This we ask in the name of Jesus Christ, our resurrected Lord. Amen**

FIFTH SUNDAY OF EASTER

O Lord God, our Maker, Redeemer, and Sanctifier, we, Your children in Christ Jesus, come before You with hearts filled with gratitude and praise. **We thank You for the power You manifested to Moses in the burning bush.** Since we are now Your chosen people in Christ Jesus, we look forward to Your leadership through the wilderness of this world to the promised land of heavenly rest.

We confess that our deeds have not always been consistent with our words. Too often we have permitted Satan to discourage us from fulfilling our good intentions. **We have allowed our hearts to condemn us, forgetting that because of our faith in Your Son Jesus Christ, You do not condemn us.** We have failed to approach You with confidence that through Christ our prayers will be answered. **For failing to keep Your commandments and still expecting You to provide for all our needs, forgive us, O Lord.**

Send us Your Holy Spirit that He may strengthen our faith. **Help us to show that we are Christians by our love.** May everything we say or do show that we abide in Christ and that He abides in us. **As branches of the true Vine Jesus Christ, may we produce the kind of fruit that You expect of us.**

Grant Your divine guidance to the leaders of our nation. **As redeemed citizens help us to work for just laws for the benefit of all.**

(*Here special intercessions, silent or spoken, may be made. If spoken, each portion concludes:* Lord, in Your mercy, **hear our prayer.**)

Give us a faith that can overcome all obstacles. **This we ask in the name of Jesus Christ, our Savior and Lord. Amen**

SIXTH SUNDAY OF EASTER

We sing a new song, O Lord, for You have done marvelous things. **Through the resurrection of Your Son Jesus Christ You have brought victory over the grave.** You have revealed that victory to reliable witnesses, who were sent forth to spread the Good News. **You have given the gift of Your Holy Spirit to both Jew and Gentile.** For using Your power in behalf of the human race, **we give You our deepest thanks.**

We confess, O Lord, that in spite of the glory which You have revealed in Your Son Jesus Christ, **we have often failed to listen to Him.** We have paid too much attention to the world and the voices of the world. **We have not always distinguished in love between the spirit of truth and the spirit of error.** By not keeping all the commandments, we have failed to show love to Him who first loved us. **We often forget that we did not choose You but that You chose us.** We have not loved one another as You loved us. **Forgive us, O Lord.**

Send us Your Holy Spirit that we may more adequately bear the fruits of Your love. **Help us to show this love impartially—even to those with whom we do not agree.** Although the world may not understand why we love, may there be no uncertainty that we truly do love. **May Your love permeate the whole world that our nation and all nations may live together in peace.** Grant us the ability to reflect Your love in all our personal relationships.

(*Here special intercessions, silent or spoken, may be made. If spoken, each portion concludes:* Lord, in Your mercy, **hear our prayer.**)

May we reflect Your love in our home, church, and state. **This we ask in the name of our resurrected Lord. Amen**

THE ASCENSION OF OUR LORD

O Lord Jesus Christ, exalted far above all principalities, power, might, and dominion, at whose name every knee should bow, not only in this world but also in the world to come, **accept our praise and adoration.**

We know that our praise cannot exalt You any higher than the position You already have at the right hand of God the Father, **yet we are bold enough to believe that You delight in the commendation of Your children.** Accept our humble thanks for giving us the privilege of being part of Your body, the Church.

For the many appearances You made after Your resurrection, proving to witnesses that You had risen from the dead, we are grateful. We also thank You for assembling so many of the faithful to witness Your ascension. **These witnesses to Your resurrection and ascension inspire us to follow You.**

As the ascended Head of the Church, O Lord, You are aware of the many problems confronting the Church today. **We do not ask that our work be made easier, but only for Your power to help us cope with the problems.** Help us to be Your hands, doing deeds of kindness. **Help us to be Your feet, running errands of mercy.** Help us to be Your mouth, witnessing to Your love and salvation.

(*Here special intercessions, silent or spoken, may be made. If spoken, each portion concludes:* Lord, in Your mercy, **hear our prayer.**)

When at last we have fulfilled Your purpose in our lives, **take us to Your ascension throne, where we may share Your glory forevermore. Amen**

SEVENTH SUNDAY OF EASTER

Almighty God, heavenly Father, we appear before You without fear because we believe You love us through Your Son Jesus Christ. **We thank and praise You for the evidence of Your love in the gift of Your Son.** We praise You for sending us Your Holy Spirit, who helps us to accept Your love. **For this undeserved love we give You heartfelt thanks.**

We confess, O Lord, that our love for You has been far from perfect. **We often forget that Your love should cast out every fear.** We have often been fearful when we should have been courageous. **We truly believe that You raised Your Son Jesus Christ from the dead, but we have been timid in witnessing to the power of His resurrection.** We have failed to give adequate witness to others so that your Holy Spirit can work faith in their hearts. **We could have been more faithful in exposing ourselves to Your Word and sacraments for the strengthening of our own faith. Forgive us, O Lord.**

Help us, O Lord, to make better use of Your Word of truth. **Enlighten our hearts that we may reflect the joy of our salvation.** Give us the courage to acknowledge that we belong to You through our Lord and Savior Jesus Christ. **May our witness quiet the fears of those who do not know You.** Help us to strengthen the weak and bring hope to the hopeless.

(*Here special intercessions, silent or spoken, may be made. If spoken, each portion concludes:* Lord, in Your mercy, **hear our prayer.**)

Help us to be friends to the friendless and a source of comfort to the sorrowful. **We pray in the name of our resurrected Lord and Savior Jesus Christ. Amen**

PENTECOST

Heavenly Father, Creator of all things great and small, **we, Your creatures, come before You with hearts filled with gratitude and praise.** As we consider the complexity of the smallest living thing and give thought to the marvelous way in which You made us, **we stand in awe of Your wisdom.** Not only have You marvelously created all things, but You have also provided for their needs; **You open Your hands and they are filled with good things.** For this Your care and providence, **we give You humble thanks.**

Since we live by the breath of Your mouth and our souls need nourishment as well as our bodies, **we are especially thankful on this day of Pentecost that You poured out the gift of Your Holy Spirit.** By His power we have become Your children through faith in Jesus Christ. **As Your children, we need constant renewal and strengthening of our faith.** As You promised through Your prophet Joel that You would pour out Your Holy Spirit on all flesh, **we ask You to include us in the fulfillment of that promise.**

As members of the Church which You began with the outpouring of the Holy Spirit, **we ask You to give us the wisdom and dedication to carry out the mission of Your Church in a manner that is pleasing to You.** Help us find those who are thirsting for the water of life.

(*Here special intercessions, silent or spoken, may be made. If spoken, each portion concludes:* Lord, in Your mercy, **hear our prayer.**)

Help us bring those who are thirsting after righteousness to Jesus, where they can quench their thirst. **We pray in the name of the Head of the Church, our Lord Jesus Christ. Amen**

THE HOLY TRINITY
First Sunday after Pentecost

God the Father, God the Son, and God the Holy Spirit, One in Three and Three in One, **accept our praise for our creation, redemption, and sanctification.**

Heavenly Father, Author of our creation, **we give you thanks for permitting us to live in Your beautiful world.** For the lofty skies, the warmth and energy of the sun, summer and winter, and day and night, **we give You thanks.** For the evidence of Your power, which is revealed in towering mountain peaks, ocean tides, the lightning of a storm, and mighty rushing winds, **we give You thanks.** For Your inestimable love, which provides for all our needs, and most of all for Your redemption of the world by our Lord and Savior Jesus Christ, **we give You thanks.**

O Jesus Christ, Author and Finisher of our faith, for redeeming us from the power of Satan, for freeing us from the slavery of sin, and for opening to us the gates of everlasting life, **accept our sincere gratitude.** For showing us how to live with people, for suffering and dying for us, for giving our lives a purpose by commissioning us to be Your witnesses, **we sing Your praises.**

O Holy Spirit, Source of our faith, for calling us by the Gospel, for enlightening us with Your gifts, for establishing the Christian Church on earth, for keeping us in the true faith, **we give You thanks.**

O Father, Son, and Holy Spirit, in the midst of all Your blessings, **we have been guilty of abusing Your gifts.** We have been wasteful of Your created resources. **We have failed to carry out Your Great Commission. Forgive us, O Lord.**

(*Here special intercessions, silent or spoken, may be made. If spoken, each portion concludes:* Lord, in Your mercy, **hear our prayer.**)

We commend ourselves to Your care. **In Jesus' name we pray. Amen**

SECOND SUNDAY AFTER PENTECOST

Lord God, our Creator, Redeemer, and Sanctifier, we acknowledge that in Your sight we are but dust and ashes. **We praise You, for we are wonderfully made; marvelous are Your works, and this our souls know right well.** We praise You for Your wisdom that ordered mankind to rest from its labor every Lord's day. **As You rested from Your work of creation, so it is our joy on our day of rest to praise You.**

We confess that we have often violated Your command to rest. **In the pursuit of earthly gain we have often taxed our strength to dangerous limits.** We forget that when we stop our work to pray, meditate, and give You thanks, we are not wasting our time. **In our feverish pursuit of earthly gain we forget that we are to live by faith in Your promise that You will provide all things needful.** We have failed to exert sufficient influence on our society to observe Your day of rest. **We have often permitted the world to influence us rather than working to influence the world.** For these and many other violations of Your divine will, we beg Your forgiveness.

May Your Holy Spirit move us to conduct our lives in a manner that will reflect our faith in Your wisdom and might. Help us to remember that You take more pleasure in our obedience than in much sacrifice. **Bless our nation.**

(*Here special intercessions, silent or spoken, may be made. If spoken, each portion concludes:* Lord, in Your mercy, **hear our prayer.**)

Bless the efforts of the Church to promote Your holy name throughout the world. **This we ask in the name of the Lord of the Sabbath, our Lord and Savior Jesus Christ. Amen**

THIRD SUNDAY AFTER PENTECOST

Lord God, heavenly Father, we come before You with thanksgiving and praise. **We praise You for our creation, preservation, and redemption.** We thank You for raising Your Son Jesus Christ from the dead and for preparing a place eternal in the heavens for all who trust in Your Son as their Savior. **For sending us Your Holy Spirit so that we might accept Jesus Christ as Lord, we give You thanks.**

We confess, O Lord, that we have often attempted to hide from You. **Our sins have often broken the lines of communication between us.** We claim to be Your children through faith in Christ, but we have often failed to do Your will. **We have not always behaved as members of Your family and have often permitted Satan to drive a wedge of division between us.** For giving the world the impression that Your kingdom is divided against itself, **forgive us, O Lord.**

May Your Holy Spirit never leave us or forsake us. **When we stray from Your fold graciously search us out and find us.** When troubles and afflictions seem greater than we can bear, **help us to remember that our mortal bodies are only the temporary dwelling place of Your Spirit.** Keep in our hearts and minds the assurance that You have built for us a house eternal in the heavens. **When the time of our departure from this earth draws near, take us to live with You eternally.**

(Here special intercessions, silent or spoken, may be made. If spoken, each portion concludes: Lord, in Your mercy, **hear our prayer.**)

We pray for our leaders in both state and church. Be with the sick, the lonely, and the depressed. **We ask these favors, O Lord, in the name of Jesus Christ, our Lord and Savior. Amen**

FOURTH SUNDAY AFTER PENTECOST

We give thanks to You, O Lord, and sing to Your name, O Most High. **You show forth Your loving-kindness every morning and Your faithfulness every night.** You have made us glad through Your Word. **We triumph in the work of Your hands.**

We confess, O Lord, that we have no righteousness of our own that should cause us to flourish as a palm tree in Your garden. **We have been negligent in sowing the seed of Your Word so that Your kingdom may increase.** We have too easily become discouraged when we do not see the seed bearing fruit. **We have often failed to believe that with Your blessing the seed of Your Word might become a great tree in Your kingdom.** For not realizing the importance of the small tasks we can perform in Your kingdom, **forgive us, O Lord.**

Grant us Your power from on high by sending us the gift of Your Holy Spirit according to Your promise. **As You have given us the power to become Your children through faith in Jesus Christ, so grant us the determination to spread Your Word.** Strengthen our faith and help us put our faith into action. **May the anticipation of the fulfillment of Your glory in us give us the zeal to accomplish Your will.** Help us see the needs of those around us, and give us the insight to be Your answer to those needs. **Strengthen the weak, and give sight to the spiritually blind.** Give the hope of healing to the sick and a reason for living to the discouraged and depressed.

(*Here special intercessions, silent or spoken, may be made. If spoken, each portion concludes:* Lord, in Your mercy, **hear our prayer.**)

Bless our nation with peace, and help us dwell in harmony with Your will. **This we ask in the name of our Lord and Savior Jesus Christ. Amen**

FIFTH SUNDAY AFTER PENTECOST

We give thanks to You, O Lord, for You are good and Your steadfast love endures forever. **Before You called us into existence, You fashioned this beautiful world for our habitation.** In Your wisdom You prescribed limits to the oceans and seas. **Your clouds carry water to a thirsty land.**

In the midst of these wonders, O Lord, we try to live our lives to Your honor and glory. **Our attempts to reflect Your glory have often ended in failure.** We are guilty of wasting Your natural resources. **We have marred the face of the earth with our waste.** You created the world so that we might live on it in peace and harmony, **but we have often been the cause of disharmony and strife.** You established Your divine laws to govern our conduct, **yet we have often transgressed Your law.** For our many transgressions and for our failure to recognize Your divine majesty, **forgive us, O Lord.**

Send us Your Holy Spirit that we may live no longer for ourselves but for Him who died for us, even our Savior Jesus Christ. **Help us to be Your new creation in Christ.** Speak peace to our souls as the winds of adversity threaten to make us afraid. **Strengthen our faith that we may believe that You will bring us safely through the storms of life.** Put Your Spirit into the hearts of our representatives in church and state. **Curb the evil influence of the wicked, and use us to maintain peace and order in our society.**

(*Here special intercessions, silent or spoken, may be made. If spoken, each portion concludes:* Lord, in Your mercy, **hear our prayer.**)

Open our eyes to the needs of others, and help us to meet those needs. **Grant our requests in the name of Your Son, our Lord and Savior Jesus Christ. Amen**

SIXTH SUNDAY AFTER PENTECOST

Your steadfast love, O Lord, never ceases, and Your mercies never come to an end. **You are good to those who wait for You, and when we truly seek You, we find You.** Therefore we sing Your praises and give thanks to Your holy name. **Your anger is for a moment and Your favor is for a lifetime.**

We confess, O Lord, that in spite of Your patience and lovingkindness, we so often take You for granted. **You answer our prayers, yet we often fail to lay before You all the burdens of our hearts.** You have given us of Your abundance, and yet we have failed to give to You and Your cause according to our means and beyond our means. **We weep at the loss of loved ones, not fully realizing that one day we shall be with them before Your throne.** We have often been afraid when we should have believed. **For our indifference and neglect, forgive us, O Lord.**

We need, O Lord, the power of Your Holy Spirit to enable us to give ourselves completely to You. **Send us Your Spirit that we may experience the joy of a life dedicated to spreading Your love.** Replace our fear with a firm trust in Your providence. **Help us to excel in fath, in utterance, in knowledge, and in all earnestness.** Help us to share our abundance with those who are in want. **Comfort the bereaved with the hope of Your promised resurrection.** Give to the sick, faith in the power of Your healing. **Assure the lonely of Your presence.**

(*Here special intercessions, silent or spoken, may be made. If spoken, each portion concludes:* Lord, in Your mercy, **hear our prayer.**)

Bless our nation with peace, and help us dwell in harmony with Your will. **This we ask in the name of our Lord and Savior Jesus Christ. Amen**

SEVENTH SUNDAY AFTER PENTECOST

Lord God, heavenly Father, by Your grace we greet another day. **For Your protection during the night, we give You thanks.** For giving us the health and strength to assemble before You in the congregation of Your redeemed, we praise Your holy name. **For refreshing us at the fountain of Your Word and Sacrament, we rejoice.**

We confess that we have often been a rebellious and stubborn people. **We have often been more concerned about Your messengers than about Your message.** We have listened to Your Word but have failed to apply it to our daily lives. **We have complained about our weaknesses and failed to lean on Your strength.** We have been impatient under trials, forgetting that through them You strengthen our faith. **We have transgressed against Your laws, knowing that You expect us to keep them.** For our sins against ourselves, against others, and against You, **forgive us, O Lord, for Jesus' sake.**

Send us Your Holy Spirit to teach us to bear with patience our own and others' infirmities. **Keep us diligent in prayer, and open our eyes to see Your answers.** May Your almighty power be the strength of our weaknesses. **Help us to believe that through our faith in Your Son Jesus Christ we can overcome all our problems.** Grant a special measure of Your Holy Spirit to Your Church that its members may be lights that shine brightly in a world of confusion and weakness.

(*Here special intercessions, silent or spoken, may be made. If spoken, each portion concludes:* Lord, in Your mercy, **hear our prayer.**)

May the leaders of our nation serve You in complete trust and honesty. **In the name of Jesus, our Lord and Savior, we pray. Amen**

EIGHTH SUNDAY AFTER PENTECOST

Heavenly Father, almighty God, we come to You in adoration and praise. **For having called us before the foundation of the world to be a part of Your kingdom, we give You thanks.** For the riches of Your grace through Your Son Jesus Christ, we praise Your most holy name. **For revealing to us the mystery of Your will, we are grateful.**

We confess that, although You destined us to be Your children through Jesus Christ, we have not always lived to the praise of His glory. **We have neglected many opportunities to bring the word of truth and knowledge of salvation to others.** For our lack of zeal for Your cause, **forgive us, O Lord.**

Send us Your promised Holy Spirit that we may be inspired to hear Your word of truth and live according to it. **Having been redeemed at the price of Your Son's blood, may we treasure this knowledge and do Your holy will.** Move us to share Your Gospel with the whole world. **Preserve the liberties we enjoy as Your children in a free land.** To this end bless the efforts of dedicated citizens to keep our nation free. **Help us to practice the freedom of religion by sharing the treasures of Your Gospel with our fellow citizens.** May the sick feel Your healing power, the lonely Your presence, and the anxious Your peace. **Protect us from demonic forces within and without our nation that we may continue to live in peace.**

(*Here special intercessions, silent or spoken, may be made. If spoken, each portion concludes:* Lord, in Your mercy, **hear our prayer.**)

Grant peace to our world, and help us to live in harmony with Your will. **We pray in the name of Jesus Christ, our Lord and Savior. Amen**

NINTH SUNDAY AFTER PENTECOST

O Lord our Righteousness, we, the sheep of Your flock, gather together to bring You our praise and thanksgiving. **We praise You for breaking down the dividing wall of hostility between us by bringing us near to You through the blood of Christ.** For making it possible for us to become fellow citizens and members of Your household, **we give You thanks.**

In spite of all Your merciful kindness, we must confess that we have often strayed from Your way like lost sheep. **We have not always heeded Your voice as it comes to us through Your undershepherds.** We have, at times, permitted ourselves to be led astray by those who are not Your shepherds. **We have not always built solidly on the foundation of the apostles and prophets with Jesus Christ as the chief cornerstone.** In His name we humbly ask Your forgiveness.

May Your Holy Spirit keep in our hearts the assurance that we always have access to Your throne. Make our hearts Your dwelling place.

Help the leaders of our nation deal wisely as they execute justice and righteousness in the land. Bless Your Church with peace and harmony and a sincere love for Your Word and sacraments. **Extend Your healing power to the sick and raise the spirits of the depressed.**

(*Here special intercessions, silent or spoken, may be made. If spoken, each portion concludes:* Lord, in Your mercy, **hear our prayer.**)

Assure the lonely of Your presence and comfort the bereaved with the hope of the resurrection. **According to Your will grant our petitions. We pray in Jesus' name. Amen**

TENTH SUNDAY AFTER PENTECOST

We extol You, O God, and bless Your name forever. **You are great, O Lord, and Your greatness is unsearchable.** You are gracious and merciful, slow to anger, and abounding in steadfast love. **Your kingdom is an everlasting kingdom, enduring through all generations.**

Our good intentions, O Lord, to do everything that You would have us do, often fall short of achievement. **We have not led a life worthy of the calling to which we have been called.** We have not always spoken the truth in love, nor have we always dealt with one another in lowliness, patience, and forbearance. **Even though it is Your desire that we maintain the unity of the spirit in the bond of peace,** we have often disturbed the peace and presented to the world a picture of disunity. **For these violations of Your precepts, forgive us, O Lord.**

With the aid of Your Holy Spirit, help us show others how You provide the essentials for our physical life as well as our spiritual life. **As You fed thousands with a few barley loaves and a few fish,** help us to believe that You will provide for our necessities. **Keep us from worrying about earthly bread, and help us seek the Bread of life.**

Keep us mindful of the needs of others, and help us to share our abundance. **Grant stability to the weather that the world's crops may be harvested in due season.** May there be peace and harmony among the nations so that the channels of communication and transport remain open.

(*Here special intercessions, silent or spoken, may be made. If spoken, each portion concludes:* Lord, in Your mercy, **hear our prayer.**)

Bless the efforts of Your Church in helping those in need. **According to Your will, grant our requests in Jesus' name. Amen**

ELEVENTH SUNDAY AFTER PENTECOST

Lord God, heavenly Father, Source of all our supply, Creator and Sustainer of our life, accept the praise of our lips and the gratitude of our hearts. **Your mercies are new every morning, and Your kindness watches over us every night.** You send us our daily bread and have given us the Bread of life in Your Son Jesus Christ. **For these constant evidences of Your love we praise Your most holy name.**

Forgive us, O Lord, when we are critical of Your leadership. **Forgive us when we murmur against Your goodness.** We have often exerted more energy in acquiring bread for our bodies than in seeking the Bread of life. **In the name of Your Son Jesus we ask Your forgiveness.**

Send us Your Holy Spirit that He may transform our old nature into Your new creation in Christ. **Remove from us deceitful lusts, which seek to satisfy the cravings of the flesh.** Renew the spirit of our minds, and put on us the new nature created after Your likeness in true righteousness and holiness. **Strengthen our faith in Jesus Christ, whom You have sent, and help us proclaim Him to the world as the Bread of life.**

Grant us good government and faithful and pious rulers. Protect us from enemies both inside and outside our nation.

(*Here special intercessions, silent or spoken, may be made. If spoken, each portion concludes:* Lord, in Your mercy, **hear our prayer.**)

Bestow Your power of healing on the sick, the assurance of Your presence on the lonely, and Your Spirit of hope on the depressed. **Grant our requests according to Your will; in the name of Jesus Christ we pray. Amen**

TWELFTH SUNDAY AFTER PENTECOST

We praise You, O Lord, in all circumstances. **We will speak of the glory of Your grace to everyone we meet.** We have put You to the test and are convinced that in everything You work for good with those who love You. **This gives us courage, for which we humbly thank and praise You.**

We confess that in spite of Your assurance of constant care, we often get discouraged with our lot in life. **When we compare ourselves with others who have done great things for You, we feel small and unimportant.** We have often grieved Your Holy Spirit. **We have often permitted circumstances to make us bitter and angry toward others.** We have not loved one another as we should. **We have failed to be imitators of Your love and forgiveness in Christ.** For our many transgressions, forgive us for the sake of Christ.

Fill us with Your Holy Spirit that we may walk in the sacrificial love with which Christ loved us. May our lives be a sweet-smelling offering of continual thanksgiving. **May we reflect to others a faith which believes that we shall live forever.** Bless our witness so that all who are taught may learn that Christ is their hope of everlasting life.

Bless our nation, O Lord, with righteousness and peace. May all those in positions of government use their influence for the greatest good of all our citizens. **Grant healing to the sick and peace of mind to the troubled.**

(*Here special intercessions, silent or spoken, may be made. If spoken, each portion concludes:* Lord, in Your mercy, **hear our prayer.**)

Give food to the hungry and the assurance of Your love to the straying and lost. **We come to You in the name of Jesus Christ, our Lord, the Bread of life. Amen**

THIRTEENTH SUNDAY AFTER PENTECOST

In praise and adoration, O Lord, we come before You, our hearts filled with gratitude. **Once again Your almighty power has brought us safely through the night.** In You, O Lord, is our trust; **You shower down on us Your kindness and mercy.**

We acknowledge, O Lord, that in spite of Your mercies we have not always walked in wisdom. **We have wasted precious time and have failed to discipline ourselves in food and drink.** We have neglected opportunities to worship with our fellow Christians in psalms, hymns, and spiritual songs. **We have murmured and complained when we should have been making melodies in our hearts to Your honor and glory.** We have failed to thank You for everything, including our adversities, which strengthen our faith. **We have sinned, O Lord; forgive us for Jesus' sake.**

Fill us with Your Holy Spirit that we may readily embrace and ever hold fast to Your Son Jesus Christ. **As He has given us His flesh to eat and His blood to drink, help us recognize in Him the source of our life.** May He abide in us and we in Him. **May our faith in Him be reflected in our lives.**

May our leaders in state and church safeguard our freedom to worship You according to Your will. **Be with the sick and comfort the bereaved with the hope of the resurrection.**

(*Here special intercessions, silent or spoken, may be made. If spoken, each portion concludes:* Lord, in Your mercy, **hear our prayer.**)

Give hope to the discouraged and lift the spirits of the depressed. **This we ask in the name of Jesus Christ. Amen**

FOURTEENTH SUNDAY AFTER PENTECOST

Praise and honor be to You, dear heavenly Father. **You have brought us through many trials to this present hour.** Your power and might have been our constant companions. **Through the righteousness of Jesus Christ, You have heard our cries for help and answered our prayers.** For Your constant care and watchfulness on our behalf, accept our praise and adoration.

We are humbly sorry for our sins, which are too many even to recall. In a world which is often confused in its judgment between right and wrong, we have not always clearly shown that we are on Your side. **Too often we have been influenced by the immorality surrounding us.** We have not loved our spouses with the same sacrificial love with which Christ loved the Church. **We have occasionally taken offense at some of the teachings of Your Son.** For our many transgressions against Your holy will, forgive us, O Lord.

May Your Holy Spirit be our constant companion. May He dwell within us always. **Help us to believe constantly that You alone have the words of eternal life.** Guide the hearts of those in authority to Your praise and glory and to the welfare of our land. **Help the sick through Your healing power.**

(*Here special intercessions, silent or spoken, may be made. If spoken, each portion concludes:* Lord, in Your mercy, **hear our prayer.**)

Give the lonely an awareness of Your presence. **Grant our petitions in the name of our Lord and Savior Jesus Christ. Amen**

FIFTEENTH SUNDAY AFTER PENTECOST

Lord God, heavenly Father, with thanksgiving and praise we come before You. **You have made known Your will in Your commandments.** You have bestowed Your blessings on those who live by faith in Christ and seek to keep Your commandments. **By our own efforts we cannot walk blamelessly before You.** But through the merits of our Lord Jesus Christ we dare approach Your holy majesty. **For making it possible to appear blameless before You, we give You humble and hearty thanks.**

We confess that we have often tried to stand in our own strength rather than trust in the strength of Your might. **We have yielded to some of Satan's temptations because we failed to put on the whole armor of God.** Our loins were not always girded with truth, nor did we always face the world with the breastplate of righteousness. **Our feet have not always been shod with the Gospel of peace, and we have often forgotten to put on the shield of faith.** Our performance as Christian soldiers has left much to be desired. **Forgive us, O Lord.**

Renew and cleanse our hearts with the sanctifying power of Your Holy Spirit. **May the hearing of Your Word and the use of Your sacraments produce in us a living faith.** May our faith show itself in deeds of love toward others, especially to those in need. **May our church and state leaders be more intent on doing Your will than pleasing people.**

(*Here special intercessions, silent or spoken, may be made. If spoken, each portion concludes:* Lord, in Your mercy, **hear our prayer.**)

May we all recognize Your hand in our afflictions that through them we may be strengthened. **We pray in Jesus' name. Amen**

SIXTEENTH SUNDAY AFTER PENTECOST

Eternal, almighty God, heavenly Father, how good it is to sing Your praises. **How delightful it is to assemble in Your house with our fellow redeemed.** You revive our hopes in a world filled with the broken promises of man. **Your Word is truth, and Your promises are sure fulfillment.** You alone have the might and power to accomplish those things which we are unable to do. **Accept our praise and thanksgiving for graciously using Your power among us.**

For trusting too much in human resources for the solutions to our problems, **forgive us, O Lord.** For being fearful when we know Your power is available for the asking, **forgive us, O Lord.** For being slow to hear, quick to speak, and quick to anger, **forgive us, O Lord.**

Open our eyes to Your goodness and to the needs of others. **Unstop our ears that we may hear Your voice above the noise and confusion of our times.** Unloose our tongues that we may speak of the wonders of Your mighty acts. **Give us vision to see the world ripe for the harvest.** May all ears be attentive to the message of Your heavenly Gospel. **May all voices be tuned to sing Your praises.**

Give insight, understanding, and vision to our nation's citizens and leaders. **Grant the inspiration of Your Holy Spirit to all church members and religious leaders.** In our families help us to listen to one another with patience.

(*Here special intercessions, silent or spoken, may be made. If spoken, each portion concludes:* Lord, in Your mercy, **hear our prayer.**)

In the name of Him who restores sight to the blind, hearing to the deaf, and speech to the dumb, **even Christ our Lord. Amen**

SEVENTEENTH SUNDAY AFTER PENTECOST

Lord God, heavenly Father, bend down Your listening ear and hear our prayer. **We bring to you our thanks and praise.** In Your mercy You answer all our sincere prayers. **We know you are ever willing to keep our eyes from tears and our feet from stumbling.** For Your continual care and concern, accept our praise and thanksgiving.

You have redeemed us to be Your own through the merits and death of Your beloved Son. Yet we have not always lived as Your redeemed children. **We have catered to the rich and often neglected the poor.** In our knowledge of justification by faith alone we have often neglected the good works that should flow from our free salvation. **We are often tempted to think that our good works deserve Your attention.** We have often permitted Satan to make us feel that our past sins are so great that You won't listen to us. **For our thoughts of self-righteousness and self-condemnation, forgive us, O Lord.**

Pour out Your Holy Spirit on us that He may help us follow Your Son Jesus Christ more closely. **Help us to deny ourselves and take up our crosses and follow Him.** Give us the courage to make sacrifices that Your Gospel might reach people both near and far. **Give us insight to understand that as we lose our life in service to You and others, we will find it.** Help us to live so that others may learn that You are a God whose presence is a reality here on earth.

(*Here special intercessions, silent or spoken, may be made. If spoken, each portion concludes:* Lord, in Your mercy, **hear our prayer.**)

May our lives reflect Your goodness. **We pray in Jesus' name. Amen**

EIGHTEENTH SUNDAY AFTER PENTECOST

Gracious God and Father of all, we, Your children in Christ Jesus, bring You our sacrifice of praise. **We praise Your name, O Lord, for it is good.** You have delivered us from the dominion of Satan so that he no longer has ultimate power over us. **You have protected us from the evil schemes of the wicked.** You have saved us with Your great power and defended us with Your might. **We praise and adore Your most holy name.**

Our attempts, O Lord, to lead a good life and show our works in all meekness of wisdom have often failed. **We have often permitted jealousy and selfish ambition to rule our hearts.** In our desire to be important we have often forgotten that You judge greatness by service. **For these and other transgressions against Your will, forgive us, O Lord.**

Grant us the gift of Your Holy Spirit that we may pattern our lives more closely to the life of our Lord Jesus Christ. **Give us that wisdom which is pure, peaceable, gentle, open to reason, full of mercy and good fruits.** Help us to live our lives in single-mindedness and sincerity. **May the harvest of our lives be one of righteousness sown in peace.**

May Your heavenly wisdom guide the leaders of our nation and church. **Bless our nation with peace, and help us dwell in harmony with Your will.** Grant the assurance of Your presence to those who bear crosses of sickness, discouragement, bereavement, or loneliness.

(*Here special intercessions, silent or spoken, may be made. If spoken, each portion concludes:* Lord, in Your mercy, **hear our prayer.**)

Bring the knowledge of salvation to the lost. **We pray in the name of Jesus Christ, our Lord. Amen**

NINETEENTH SUNDAY AFTER PENTECOST

Lord God, heavenly Father, we are filled with awe and wonder as we consider Your marvelous works. **Your goodness has blessed us with refreshing sleep, and Your kindness awakens us to the miracle of life.** You have put our conscience at ease when we recall that all our sins are forgiven for the sake of Your Son Jesus Christ. **Such grace is too wonderful for us to understand: we are overcome with praise and adoration for Your most holy name.**

It saddens us that in the midst of Your gracious blessings we should ever transgress Your holy will. **In spite of Your continual care and concern, we know that we have sinned.** We have envied those who seem to have a greater measure of Your Holy Spirit. **We have misjudged the Christianity of some who are not members of our group.** We have offended little children with thoughtless remarks and undisciplined living. **We have often failed to show by our life just what a Christian ought to be.** For these and all our offenses against Your holy will and against others, **forgive us, O Lord, for Jesus' sake.**

Pour out Your Holy Spirit on us that we may more accurately reflect Your glory in a sin-filled world. **Help us to exert a Christian influence in the affairs of state and church.**

(*Here special intercessions, silent or spoken, may be made. If spoken, each portion concludes:* Lord, in Your mercy, **hear our prayer.**)

Help us to bring Your strength of healing to the sick, Your hope to the discouraged, and Your presence to the lonely. **Hear our prayer, O Lord, for the sake of Jesus Christ, our Savior. Amen**

TWENTIETH SUNDAY AFTER PENTECOST

We thank and praise You, heavenly Father, for all the spiritual blessings and human joys You continually shower upon us. **For adopting us through Christ to be members of Your heavenly family, we give You thanks.** For permitting us to live in the companionship of our earthly family, **we praise Your holy name.**

You have established the family as the first and most important unit of our society. **But we must confess that we have not always treasured the members of our family as highly as we ought.** As husband and wife we have not always treated one another with the kindness and consideration You would expect of those who claim Jesus Christ as Savior. **We may have even thought of leaving our spouses for reasons that You would not condone.** As parents we have not always done our best to bring up our children in Your nurture and admonition. **For all the sins that we have committed, we ask Your divine forgiveness.**

Grant the gift of Your Holy Spirit to each member of our family that we may live in the spirit of love and forgiveness. **May Your Spirit also permeate the hearts of all who are members of Your spiritual family, the Church.** Grant wisdom and understanding to our nation's leaders in all branches of government, that our laws and the interpretation of those laws may help preserve the family in our society.

(*Here special intercessions, silent or spoken, may be made. If spoken, each portion concludes:* Lord, in Your mercy, **hear our prayer.**)

We ask these petitions, O heavenly Father, **in the name of Your Son Jesus Christ, our Brother and Savior. Amen**

TWENTY-FIRST SUNDAY AFTER PENTECOST

Eternal, everlasting God and Father of Jesus the Christ, we come before You with praise and thanksgiving. **Through all the years of our life You have provided all our physical needs and kept us in the Christian faith.** For our physical and spiritual preservation we give You thanks. **We are fearfully and wonderfully made; marvelous are all Your works. Accept, O Lord, our heartfelt praise.**

As descendants of the first human pair whom You created in Your image of righteousness and true holiness, we, like they, have lost that image. **While we are grateful for all Your mercies, we know that we have sinned.** Much of the precious time You have granted us, we have wasted in pursuing the wrong goals. **O Lord, we have been so preoccupied with seeking earthly treasures that we have often forgotten the needs of Your kingdom.** Because the needs of the poor are not always before us, we often forget to share with them our abundance. **Sometimes we are so occupied with our families that we may neglect the needs of Your kingdom.** For not accepting the challenges to spread Your kingdom when that would require a sacrifice on our part, **forgive us, O Lord.**

Help us to number our days and apply our hearts to Your divine wisdom. **Grant an atmosphere of peace in all nations that Your Gospel may have free course to the ends of the earth.**

(*Here special intercessions, silent or spoken, may be made. If spoken, each portion concludes:* Lord, in Your mercy, **hear our prayer.**)

Help us to divide Your Word of truth properly and bring the knowledge of salvation to others. **We pray in the name of Your Son Jesus Christ, our Lord. Amen**

TWENTY-SECOND SUNDAY AFTER PENTECOST

Almighty God, our Fortress and Defense and our Shelter from the storm, accept our thanks and praise for Your divine protection amid the dangers of our earthly life. **You answer when we call; You have been with us in trouble; and You have granted us a full life.**

Of primary importance, You sent Your Suffering Servant, Jesus Christ, to rescue us from the punishment of our sins. **You bruised Him and put Him to grief.** You appointed Him to be our High Priest, who gave Himself as the offering for our sin. **By Him as many as believe are accounted righteous in Your sight because He bore our iniquities.** For all this it is our duty to thank and praise, serve and obey Him. **This is most certainly true.**

Forgive us, O Lord, for having often exalted ourselves and forgotten that the most important positions in Your kingdom go to those who consider themselves servants. **Send us Your Holy Spirit that He may keep us humble and willing to do Your will.** Help us to overcome our feelings of jealousy and envy against those whom You have placed in positions of honor.

Keep us willing to submit to those whom You have placed in authority in church and state. In our families help us be servants to one another. **Equip us to serve the sick, the lonely, and the spiritually distressed.** In all kinds of afflictions keep us in the faith of Your Son Jesus Christ, our Savior.

(*Here special intercessions, silent or spoken, may be made. If spoken, each portion concludes:* Lord, in Your mercy, **hear our prayer.**)

Grant peace to the nations of the world; **we pray in Jesus' name. Amen**

TWENTY-THIRD SUNDAY AFTER PENTECOST

Glory, honor, and praise be to You, Lord God of heaven and earth. **When we consider Your heavens, the sun, the moon, the stars, and the planets, we are amazed that You would pay any attention to us.** Yet, according to Your Word, You determined our destiny before You laid the foundation of the earth. **Most amazing of all is that You provided for our salvation from the very beginning that we might one day enter into Your rest.** Accept our sincere thanks and praise.

We confess that there have been times when we have forgotten Your merciful kindness toward us. We have often been blind toward Your marvelous works. **We have read and listened to Your Word, yet failed to respond with truly believing hearts.** We have lagged in zeal in bringing the Good News of Your salvation to all the spiritually blind. **We have often stopped working before finishing the task You have called us to do.** For these and many other offenses against Your holy will, **forgive us, O Lord.**

Send us Your Holy Spirit that He may keep our eyes open to Your merciful kindness. **Give us vision to see our duty in the broader concepts of Your kingdom.** Help us recognize the opportunities to serve others. **Let us see our neighbors' needs, and give us wisdom and strength to meet those needs.**

(*Here special intercessions, silent or spoken, may be made. If spoken, each portion concludes:* Lord, in Your mercy, **hear our prayer.**)

Give vision and insight to the leaders of church and state. **Accept our prayer for the sake of Jesus Christ, our Savior. Amen**

TWENTY-FOURTH SUNDAY AFTER PENTECOST

O Lord, our Lord, You are the one and only true God. **With our hearts, minds, souls, and strength, we laud and magnify Your holy name.** For giving us laws to safeguard the happiness and well-being of the human race, **we give You thanks.** For the gift of life and the hope of everlasting life, **we adore Your divine majesty.**

We confess that we have not always loved You with all our heart, soul, and mind. **Nor have we always loved our neighbor as ourselves.** In fact, O Lord, we often find it difficult to love even ourselves, especially when we realize how often we have broken Your laws and acted contrary to Your will. **But You are a gracious Father, willing to forgive if we will but come to You in the name of our Savior Jesus Christ.** We come to You now in the faith that You have accepted His payment for the punishment of our sins. **For our many transgressions and failures to show You our love, forgive us, O Lord.** For the many times we have depreciated ourselves even though You call us Your sons and daughters, **forgive us, Lord.** For not responding wholeheartedly to the needs of our neighbor, **forgive us, O Lord.**

Send Your Holy Spirit into our hearts, minds, and souls that we may truly appreciate how good You have been to us. **Help us so to live that others may recognize your image in our life and behavior.**

(*Here special intercessions, silent or spoken, may be made. If spoken, each portion concludes:* Lord, in Your mercy, **hear our prayer.**)

Because of our witness may others desire to live according to Your will and receive Your Son Jesus Christ as their Savior. **This we ask through Jesus Christ, our Savior. Amen**

TWENTY-FIFTH SUNDAY AFTER PENTECOST

Gracious Lord, we give thanks to You for You are good and Your steadfast love endures forever. **You send rain where it is needed and clear skies to permit gathering in the harvest.** Although there may be floods and droughts, You provide a balance in nature so that we seldom lack food and drink. **For Your constant care of the human race we lift our hearts in thanksgiving.**

We confess that in spite of Your bountiful supply, we often complain because we think we need more physical comforts. **Having food and clothing, help us to be content.** Forgive our selfishness, which keeps us from giving back to You and Your kingdom a proper portion of Your gifts. **Help us to believe that if we seek first Your kingdom and its righteousness, You will provide for our necessities.** Forgive us for our frequent lack of trust in Your goodness and mercy.

Accept our thanks for giving us a high priest in Your Son Jesus Christ. Because of His sacrifice You have put away our sin and we need not fear the Day of Judgment. **With faith in His atonement, we now eagerly await His Second Coming.** Keep us in the faith so that we can welcome that event with joy.

Until that time arrives, O Lord, we are still pilgrims on this earth. Bless our nation and the nations of the world with peace.

(*Here special intercessions, silent or spoken, may be made. If spoken, each portion concludes:* Lord, in Your mercy, **hear our prayer.**)

In the name of and for the sake of Jesus Christ, Your Son and our Savior, **hear our prayer. Amen**

THIRD-LAST SUNDAY IN THE CHURCH YEAR

O merciful Father, You are a refuge for us in time of trouble. **Apart from You we are worthless.** As long as You are before us, we shall not be moved. **Our hearts are glad and our souls rejoice because in You is our security.** In Your presence is fullness of joy and in Your right hand are pleasures forevermore.

Your prophets of old and Your Son Jesus Christ have warned us of great troubles coming to the world. There will be wars and rumors of war and religious leaders arising who, claiming to be the Christ, will attempt to lead the elect astray. **There will be earthquakes and famines.** Christians will be persecuted and brought to trial because of their faith. **Members of families will be divided in their loyalties and in conflict with each other.**

Many of these prophecies have already been fulfilled, and we recognize, O Lord, that You have graciously spared many of us in our generation from these calamities. **If in Your wisdom You should determine that we suffer more in this generation,** give us the strength to endure to Your honor and glory. **Keep us in Your grace that we may be ready in the unknown hour.** As we confess our many transgressions, give us the assurance that You will remember our sins no more. **Prepare our nation to meet with courage the days that are ahead.** Help Your Church to carry out its mission of bringing the Gospel to every living creature. **Help the lonely feel Your presence.**

(*Here special intercessions, silent or spoken, may be made. If spoken, each portion concludes:* Lord, in Your mercy, **hear our prayer.**)

Grant these petitions according to Your will. **We ask in the name of Jesus Christ, our Savior. Amen**

SECOND-LAST SUNDAY IN THE CHURCH YEAR

In the congregation of those made righteous through Christ we praise You, O Lord, with our whole heart. **Your great works are full of honor and majesty.** You have sent redemption to Your people because You are gracious and merciful. **Your praise endures forever.**

Through Your Word, which will not pass away, we learn that Judgment Day is fast approaching. **Help us to recognize the signs that will precede Christ's coming.** With the assurance that all our sins are forgiven in Christ, we can approach that day with peace of heart and quietness of mind. **We know that You have entered our names in the Book of Life by the death and resurrection of Your Son Jesus Christ.**

Send us Your Holy Spirit that He may keep us alert to the rapid flight of time. **Help us to accomplish something for You in this world before You call us from it.** Because You have brought us the knowledge of salvation, for which we are grateful, grant us the opportunity to share this knowledge with others. **Help us to recognize opportunities to share Your Gospel, and give us the courage to do it.**

As You have brought again from the dead our Lord and Savior Jesus Christ, so equip us with everything to do His will. **We look forward to the day when Your angels will gather the elect from the four winds.** Grant, O Lord, that on that day we may be found among the elect.

(*Here special intercessions, silent or spoken, may be made. If spoken, each portion concludes:* Lord, in Your mercy, **hear our prayer.**)

We pray for those who need Your help in body, soul, or mind. **In the name of Him who will be the final Judge of all, we humbly pray. Amen**

LAST SUNDAY IN THE CHURCH YEAR
Sunday of the Fulfillment

Lord God, heavenly Father, hear our voices and let Your ears be attentive to our supplications. **If You would hold our sins against us, we would not be able to stand before You.** We know there is forgiveness with You, and therefore we hope in Your Word. **You have assured us of Your steadfast love in providing redemption through Your Son Jesus Christ.**

According to Your Word the end of all things on earth will come speedily. **Though the heavens vanish like smoke and the earth wear out like a garment, we will not fear.** We have Your promise of deliverance and salvation forever.

Send us Your Holy Spirit to keep us in the faith. Increase our zeal and concern for the salvation of others. **Help us to convince the doubters and win for Christ those who are headed for destruction.** Since we do not know the day or the hour when the Son of Man will return visibly to this earth as Judge, help us to be constantly prepared to meet Him. **Keep us watchful and alert.**

Until the time of Your Son's final coming, keep our world in Your grace. **Protect our nation from enemies both from within and without.** Bless the efforts of our leaders to establish and maintain peace among nations. **Give to all leaders in state and church a clear understanding of Your will.**

Extend Your healing hand to the sick, Your presence to the lonely, and Your hope to the discouraged.

(*Here special intercessions, silent or spoken, may be made. If spoken, each portion concludes:* Lord, in Your mercy, **hear our prayer.**)

Bless our nation with peace, and help us to dwell in harmony with Your will. **Help Your Church to carry out the Great Commission. In Jesus' name we pray. Amen**

LAST SUNDAY IN THE CHURCH YEAR
Sunday of the Fulfillment (Alternate)

King of the universe, Redeemer of the world, without beginning and without end, we come before You to praise Your divine majesty. **Lord Jesus Christ, we give You humble and hearty thanks for calling us into Your kingdom.** We gratefully acknowledge the benevolence of Your kingdom. **For setting aside Your divine majesty and becoming one of us, we adore Your most holy name.** For sacrificing Your life for our salvation, **we give You thanks.** You have freed us from our sins by Your blood and made us a kingdom of priests before God. **To You we ascribe glory and dominion forever.**

We know we are unworthy of the high calling that You have bestowed on us. **Our loyalty as Your subjects often leaves much to be desired.** We have Your witness to the truth in Your Word, yet we have not always been truthful. **By Your suffering and death, resurrection and ascension You have demonstrated Your love for us.** We have often been negligent in presenting Your truth that others too may come into Your kingdom. **For our lack of loyalty and zeal in spreading Your kingdom, forgive us, Lord.**

Grant us the sevenfold gifts of Your Spirit that we may more adequately function as representatives of Your truth. **Help us lead our own nation and the nations of the world to serve You.** As Lord of the forces of nature, we ask You to use Your power to relieve the suffering of the sick and restore clear thinking to distorted minds.

(*Here special intercessions, silent or spoken, may be made. If spoken, each portion concludes:* Lord, in Your mercy, **hear our prayer.**)

Keep us in the faith that one day we will see You face to face **and live and reign with You forever. Amen**

PRAYERS FOR SUNDAYS AND MAJOR FESTIVALS

Series C

FIRST SUNDAY IN ADVENT

We lift up our souls to You, O Lord. **Make us to know Your ways and teach us Your paths.** Lead us in Your truth and teach us, for You are the God of our salvation. **O holy Father, we humbly implore You, help us believe Your promises.** As Your servant Israel anticipated the coming of the Messiah, the Deliverer, **help us to recognize Jesus Christ as that Messiah and welcome Him into our hearts by faith.**

Lead us by Your Holy Spirit to an understanding of our sinfulness and our need of repentance. **Help us to hate sin and love righteousness.** Be our strength in the hour of temptation and help us to serve You and bring glory to Your name. **Send the light of the Gospel to the ends of the earth that all may know Your love in Jesus Christ.** Increase the number of those who can confess with sincerity and conviction: **blessed is He who comes in the name of the Lord! Hosanna in the highest.** May such faith enable all nations to melt their weapons of war into instruments of peace.

Grant Your abiding peace to all who are gathered in Your house today. To those among us who are afflicted, grant them strength to bear their burdens. **Give us all patience to await the joy of Your abiding presence.**

(*Here special intercessions, silent or spoken, may be made. If spoken, each portion concludes:* Lord, in Your mercy, **hear our prayer.**)

Especially, O Lord, we implore You to look with favor upon our land. **Grant wisdom, understanding, and honesty to those who govern and those who are governed.** Help us to recognize the signs of Your coming and be prepared for that great day. **We pray in the name of and for the sake of our Lord Jesus Christ. Amen**

SECOND SUNDAY IN ADVENT

Almighty God, everlasting Father, we are grateful for the great things You have done for us. **Foremost of these is bringing us into Your kingdom through Your Son Jesus.** We thank You for Your messenger John the Baptist, who, even today through Your Word, reminds us that we need to be prepared to meet Your Son at His Second Coming. **Help us not to fear Christ's sudden appearing, but keep us ready by daily repentance.**

Send us, O Lord, Your Holy Spirit that He may help us prepare Your way. **Help us to straighten the paths that all may find You.** Help us to remove those obstacles in our life which prevent others from seeing You in us. **May Your love abound in us more and more with knowledge and discernment.** Help us to approve only that which is excellent, pure, and blameless for the day of Christ. **Fill us with the fruits of righteousness which come to us through Jesus Christ, our Lord.**

Help everyone everywhere realize that as citizens of every nation accept Your Son Jesus Christ as Lord and Savior, there will be peace on earth. **Enable us to live as Your children and spread the Good News of salvation to the ends of the earth.** Direct, sanctify, and govern our lives so that they are a credit to You and the Gospel we proclaim. **Be with those who cannot be with us today.** Be with those who are in need of Your help. **Assure the lonely of Your presence.**

(*Here special intercessions, silent or spoken, may be made. If spoken, each portion concludes:* Lord, in Your mercy, **hear our prayer.**)

According to Your will, O Lord, **grant our requests in the name of Jesus Christ, our Savior. Amen**

THIRD SUNDAY IN ADVENT

We come with happy hearts, O Lord Most High, into the courts of Zion. **Your judgments against us have been removed by Him whose birth we soon shall celebrate.**

We confess that we deserve the same righteous judgments John the Baptist hurled against the multitude that came to him. **As they took too much pride in being the seed of Abraham, so we have often been too proud of our national and religious heritage.** You have abundantly blessed us with many possessions, but we have not always shared them with the needy. **You have abundantly blessed us with food, but we have not been concerned about the hungry.** As stewards of Your natural resources, we have often been guilty of wastefulness and greed. **For these and other transgressions, we ask Your divine forgiveness.**

We rejoice in Your mercy and in the assurance of forgiveness offered in Your Word and sacraments. **Help us treasure the means of Your grace, through which the Holy Spirit preserves us in the true faith.** Use us to bring these means of grace to the spiritually and physically sick. **Send Your Holy Spirit to those whom we have elected to govern us that they may use their power for the benefit of all.**

(*Here special intercessions, silent or spoken, may be made. If spoken, each portion concludes:* Lord, in Your mercy, **hear our prayer.**)

Grant Your peace to all who celebrate the birthday of Your Son. **We pray in His name. Amen**

FOURTH SUNDAY IN ADVENT

We rejoice, O heavenly Father, that You have stirred up Your might and have come to save us. **Our spiritual eyes turn toward Bethlehem, the birthplace of Your Son, as foretold by the prophet Micah.** We accept with joy the fulfillment of Your prophecy. **As John the Baptist recognized Your Son before He was born, help us also to recognize Him as Your Son and our Savior.** In a most marvelous manner You prepared a sacrifice for our sins in the womb of the Virgin Mary. **Send us Your Holy Spirit that we may truly believe and accept this miracle of Your love.** As we anticipate with joy the celebration of His birth, **grant us Your grace that we may see in Him the embodiment of Your love for us.**

Grant that all principalities and powers on this earth may welcome Your Son as their Lord. **To this end bless all communication media that carry the message of the Christmas Gospel.** Bless the governments who honor Your Son by celebrating His birth. **Help them see in Your gesture of peace toward humanity an example for peace among all nations.** Especially bless with peace, hope, and joy the homes where Jesus' birth is celebrated. **May the sick and the lonely be assured of Your presence.**

(*Here special intercessions, silent or spoken, may be made. If spoken, each portion concludes:* Lord, in Your mercy, **hear our prayer.**)

In thanks for the Gift that neither word nor tongue can fully describe, O heavenly Father, we pray that this Gift may remain ours by grace through faith. **May we know the joy of His presence. This we ask in Jesus' name. Amen**

THE NATIVITY OF OUR LORD

Praise, honor, and glory to You, O Lord our God. **With angels and archangels we magnify Your name: "Glory to God in the highest, and on earth peace among men with whom He is pleased."** We adore Your divine goodness and praise You for sending deliverance to Zion and for including us in the fulfillment of Your promises.

Even though we have no merit or worthiness within us, You have again this Christmas assured us of Your love. Instead of justly punishing us, You have sent us salvation in the birth of Your Son. **In spite of our many transgressions You have made salvation possible in this gift of mercy.**

For rejoicing more in earthbound gifts than in Your heavensent gift, forgive us, O Lord. **For telling others more about earthly treasures than about the heavenly Word made flesh, forgive us, O Lord.** Accept our thanks for the eternal gift conceived out of Your love for the world. **Accept our thanks, O Lord, for bringing the knowledge of this divine truth to us.**

Bless, O Lord, the musicians, singers, and messengers who help us rejoice in Your Son's birth. **Bless the reception of this Good News in the hearts of those who hear it.** Bless, O Lord, the spread of the Christmas message throughout the world. **May these glad tidings bring hope to the discouraged and peace to the troubled.** May the lonely see in the Christmas message the assurance of Your presence.

(*Here special intercessions, silent or spoken, may be made. If spoken, each portion concludes:* Lord, in Your mercy, **hear our prayer.**)

May the peace of Christmas fill our nation and the nations of the world. **This we ask in the name of our Savior, Christ, the Lord. Amen**

FIRST SUNDAY AFTER CHRISTMAS

Glory, honor, and praise be to You, O heavenly Father, for sending Your Son, who became like us. **Being true God, He did not consider Himself too far above us to take upon Himself our flesh and be called our Brother.** Being above all angels and laws by right of His divine origin, He, nevertheless, already as an infant, submitted to the laws intended for us. **That He should become both sacrifice and priest is a wonder too great for us to understand.**

We confess, O heavenly Father, that we are not worthy of Your consideration. **The laws You gave us to keep, we have broken.** We have been impatient in waiting for the fulfillment of Your promises; we have failed to rejoice in Your mercy. **For these and other transgressions, forgive us, O Lord.**

Grant us, O Lord, a proper understanding of our mission in life. **Strengthen us by Your Spirit to fulfill it.** Bless our feeble efforts to hold high the light of Your truth. **To this end may all nations rally under the banner of the Prince of peace and find in Him the Source of their strength.**

(Here special intercessions, silent or spoken, may be made. If spoken, each portion concludes: Lord, in Your mercy, **hear our prayer.**)

Maintain, O Lord, peace on our city streets, justice in our courts, and love in our homes. **All this we ask in the name of and for the sake of Jesus Christ, our Lord and Savior. Amen**

SECOND SUNDAY AFTER CHRISTMAS

O God and Father of our Lord Jesus Christ, who has blessed us with every spiritual blessing in Christ, **we praise and adore You for choosing us in Him before the foundation of the world.** We cannot understand how this is possible, but we believe it because of the clear testimony of Your Word. **You destined us in love to be Your children through Christ, according to the purpose of Your will.**

You have chosen us, O Lord, that we should be holy and blameless before You. **Because of the weakness of our flesh, however, we are unable to achieve Your purpose.** But thanks be to You, for through Your Son Jesus Christ You have made us holy and blameless. **He took upon Himself our flesh and dwelt among us.** He has revealed Your glory as a light shining in the darkness. **From His fullness of glory we have received Your grace.** Now we know that we can stand before You in His righteousness. **For this, Your grace and mercy, accept our humble thanks.**

As You sent John the Baptist to point to the Light, which shines in the darkness, so also empower us with Your Spirit to bear witness to that Light. **You have given us power to receive Him, to believe in His name, and thereby become Your children.** For the grace and truth we have received through Him, **we give you humble thanks.**

(*Here special intercessions, silent or spoken, may be made. If spoken, each portion concludes:* Lord, in Your mercy, **hear our prayer.**)

In the name of Him whose light still shines to all the world for the salvation of many, **we pray. Amen**

THE EPIPHANY OF OUR LORD

Dear heavenly Father, in the darkness of this world's spiritual night, You created a special star to guide the Wise Men to Your Son. **For this revelation of Your glory, we give You humble thanks.** For predicting this event through Your prophet Isaiah, hundreds of years before it took place, **we praise and adore You.**

Like Herod, we have often been guilty of being insincere in our search for Christ. **Forgive us, O Lord.** We have often failed to show others the way to Him, who is the Truth and the Light. **Have mercy on us, O Lord.** We confess that we have not always permitted Your Son to be the Light of our life. **Forgive us, O Lord.**

For guiding Gentiles to the birthplace of Your Son Jesus and for accepting their worship as fellow heirs and partakers of the promise in Christ Jesus through the Gospel, **we give You thanks.** For making it possible for us to become Your children through Christ, **we are eternally grateful.**

Send us Your Holy Spirit that He may increase our understanding of the magnitude of Your love. **Loosen our tongues and give us courage to tell the Good News to a world still largely in darkness.** Motivate us to generosity in bringing our gifts for the extension of Your kingdom. **Extend Your healing hand to the sick and Your presence to the lonely.**

(*Here special intercessions, silent or spoken, may be made. If spoken, each portion concludes:* Lord, in Your mercy, **hear our prayer.**)

Grant our government and the governments of the world sincere, honest, and wise officials. **We bring these our petitions in the name of Jesus Christ, our Lord and Savior. Amen**

THE BAPTISM OF OUR LORD
First Sunday after the Epiphany

Lord God Almighty, Source of all energy and power, we come before You in awe and wonder. **No power on earth is strong enough to cleanse us from a single sin and make us worthy to stand in Your holy presence.** But through Baptism You have washed away our sin and made us Your children by the power of the Holy Spirit. **We thank You for making it possible for us to appear before Your throne of grace without fear.**

We confess that we are not worthy of such consideration. **We confess that we failed to live up to our high calling in Christ.** We confess that we have often resisted the power of the Holy Spirit. **We confess that we have often looked elsewhere for power to run our lives.**

Forgive us, O Lord, for our neglect of Your Word and sacraments. **Forgive us, O Lord, for forgetting that they are the means through which Your power comes to us.** Forgive us, O Lord, for failing to share Your divine power with others.

As You anointed Your Son with the Holy Spirit at His baptism, so send a special measure of Your Holy Spirit to us. Empower us to bring Your Gospel to those who are still outside Your family circle. **May Your presence be a source of strength to the weak, a companion to the lonely, and a ray of hope to the discouraged.**

(*Here special intercessions, silent or spoken, may be made. If spoken, each portion concludes:* Lord, in Your mercy, **hear our prayer.**)

Grant wisdom and understanding to church and state leaders. **This we ask in the name of Jesus Christ. Amen**

SECOND SUNDAY AFTER THE EPIPHANY

Lord God, heavenly Father, Creator of light, we raise our voices to You through the darkness of night. **We praise You for Your Holy Spirit, who called us out of darkness into the light of Your understanding and wisdom.** We thank You especially that through Your Holy Spirit we can now call Jesus Christ, our Lord. **We thank You for the diversified gifts given to Your Church by the same Spirit.** As members of Christ's body, we now have the privilege of serving You and others with unity of purpose.

We confess, O Lord, that we have not always used the diversity of spiritual gifts for the extension of Your kingdom. We confess that we have become envious of those whose spiritual gifts seem greater than ours. **We confess, that we have often used the many gifts of others to excuse our failure to use the one gift we may have.** For these and many other offenses, forgive us, O Lord.

As Your Son was a welcome presence at the wedding in Cana, so help us to welcome His presence at both joyful and sad occasions. When we drink the cup of affliction and sorrow, help us remember the wine of gladness You have reserved for us in the heavenly mansions. **May the joy of our salvation spill over into our community and nation so that others may be attracted to our fellowship in Christ.**

(Here special intercessions, silent or spoken, may be made. If spoken, each portion concludes: Lord, in Your mercy, **hear our prayer.**)

To this end bless our congregation and church body in fulfilling the purpose for which You have made us members of the body of Christ. **In His name we pray. Amen**

THIRD SUNDAY AFTER THE EPIPHANY

Blessed be your name forevermore, O Lord. **From the rising of the sun to the setting of it, we praise You, O God.** You are high above all the nations and Your glory above the heavens. **As we observe the glories of the heavens, we see the imprint of Your almighty hand.**

The revelation of Your glory and majesty makes us realize how insignificant we sinful mortals really are. **We wonder with the psalmist, "What is man that You are mindful of him and the Son of Man that You visit Him?"** Yet You did visit us in the person of Jesus Christ. **For this we give You humble and hearty thanks.**

Words fail us when we try to express to You our praise. **The good tidings that You will forgive and forget our sins when we come to You in Your Son's name is music to our ears.** We confess that we have often mourned when we should have rejoiced. **Forgive us, O Lord, and accept our thanks for sending us Your Son Jesus Christ.**

He has bound up the brokenhearted, freed us from slavery to sin, and given us the oil of gladness and mantle of praise for the faint spirit. **In gratitude for such mercies may we be Your feet to carry Your Word to others, Your hands to help in time of need, and Your mouth to speak the Good News.**

(*Here special intercessions, silent or spoken, may be made. If spoken, each portion concludes:* Lord, in Your mercy, **hear our prayer.**)

May the world in which we live be moved to respond favorably to our testimony. **In Jesus' name we pray. Amen**

FOURTH SUNDAY AFTER THE EPIPHANY

O Lord God, heavenly Father, in You do we put our trust. **From the day of our birth to the present, Your goodness and righteousness have never failed us.** From the days of our youth You have taught us to know You. **Therefore we come into Your presence with great confidence, believing You will hear us.**

You have entrusted the Word of Your salvation to apostles, prophets, and teachers. **You have inspired them to write and speak Your words in many different languages that the world may know of Your truth and love.** Now that precious Word has been entrusted to us that we may daily demonstrate Your love. **Forgive us for our neglect in studying and speaking Your Word.**

It is Your desire that everything we do or say be motivated by love. **We may have helped the poor, but been too proud of our generosity.** We may have considered the welfare of others, but not at great expense to ourselves. **We have often ascribed wrong motives to the very generous and envied them when they were honored for their good works.** We have often been puffed up with pride when we compared ourselves with others. **In words, acts, and speech we have often failed to love. Forgive us, O Lord.** Send us Your Holy Spirit to help us love as You love us. **As You showed Your sacrificial love in sending Your Son, so may our lives reflect that love.**

(*Here special intercessions, silent or spoken, may be made. If spoken, each portion concludes:* Lord, in Your mercy, **hear our prayer.**)

May the sick feel Your love through Your healing hand; and the lonely, Your comforting presence. **In Jesus' name we pray. Amen**

FIFTH SUNDAY AFTER THE EPIPHANY

Holy, holy, holy, are You, O Lord of hosts; the whole world is full of Your glory. **Day unto day utters speech, and Your voice can be heard everywhere.** We are people of unclean lips, yet for the sake of Your mercy and truth, hear us. **We come to You in the righteousness of our King, Jesus Christ.**

We have heard You ask, "Whom shall I send?" **Too often we have pretended not to hear.** Too often when we said, "Here am I, send me," we did not mean it. **Too often we have loved our comforts and conveniences, inwardly fearing that You might send us.** We have failed to leave our nest of worldly goods and follow You. **We have become discouraged too easily and given up too readily in our search for lost souls.** We have used our inability to speak as a reason to discontinue the search. **In the name of Him whom we profess, even Jesus Christ our Lord, we ask You to touch our lips and take away our guilt.**

Send us Your Holy Spirit, O Lord. **Help us to see Your purpose in our lives and for the world.** Fill our hearts with Your holy fire that we might show You our thanks by doing Your will. **Use us to lead someone to Your light.**

Bless our nation's president with wisdom and insight, help our congress to fashion laws according to Your will, and cause our judicial system to administer justice to all.

(*Here special intercessions, silent or spoken, may be made. If spoken, each portion concludes:* Lord, in Your mercy, **hear our prayer.**)

Grant peace to our nation, and help us to do Your will. **This we ask in Jesus' name. Amen**

SIXTH SUNDAY AFTER THE EPIPHANY

O Lord God, heavenly Father, our Provider and Benefactor, **we praise You for the abundance of Your mercy.** Even though we do not deserve it, You daily supply our every need. **You have remained true to Your Word.** Ever since Your promise to Noah, seedtime and harvest, cold and heat, summer and winter, day and night have not ceased. **How thankful we are, O Lord, that You have been true to our trust.** For filling all our physical and spiritual needs, **we give You hearty thanks.**

We confess, O Lord, that we have not always trusted You as we should. **When we hear of threatening famines in many parts of the world, we fear for the safety of our abundance.** As we learn of others becoming unemployed, we fear the loss of our jobs. **As we experience energy shortages, we begin to distrust those in responsible positions.** We confess that we have often placed blame without being fully informed. **We are guilty of wasting many of our resources.** We have often been indifferent to the physical and spiritual needs of others. **For these and other sins, we beg Your forgiveness.**

Help us, O Lord, to be Your instruments for feeding the poor and hungry that they too may rejoice. **Help us to bring the Gospel of Your Son's resurrection to those who weep.**

Help us, O Lord, to overcome this world and its hatred with Your love. **Help us witness to others that they too may have the joyful certainty of resurrection and life eternal.**

(*Here special intercessions, silent or spoken, may be made. If spoken, each portion concludes:* Lord, in Your mercy, **hear our prayer.**)

Bless our nation with peace, and grant peace among the nations of the world. **We pray in the name of Him who is the Resurrection and the Life, Jesus Christ. Amen**

SEVENTH SUNDAY AFTER THE EPIPHANY

We bless You, O Lord, and all that is within us blesses Your holy name. **We remember all Your benefits.** You forgive our iniquities and heal our diseases. **You redeem our lives from destruction and crown us with steadfast love and mercy.** You satisfy us with good things so that our youth is renewed like the eagle's. **You are merciful, gracious, and slow to anger.** You do not deal with us according to our sins nor repay us according to our iniquities. **As high as the heavens are above the earth, so great is Your steadfast love toward us.** As far as the east is from the west, so far do You remove our transgressions from us. **For all these Your benefits we give You our humble and hearty thanks.**

We confess that we have not always returned Your love with adequate consideration for those with whom we live and work. **Instead of extending love to our enemies, we have often permitted the spirit of revenge to govern us.** We often confine our friendliness and helpfulness only to those who have been good to us. **We have passed judgment and condemnation on others.** We have not been as forgiving to others as You have been to us. **For our frequent betrayal of Your love to us, forgive us, O Lord.**

(Here special intercessions, silent or spoken, may be made. If spoken, each portion concludes: Lord, in Your mercy, **hear our prayer.**)

Visit the sick with Your healing power, the lonely with Your presence, and the bereaved with Your comfort. **We ask this in the name of our Lord and Savior Jesus Christ. Amen**

EIGHTH SUNDAY AFTER THE EPIPHANY

We give thanks to You, O Lord, and sing praises to Your most holy name. **Your steadfast love continues from morning through night.** You are the cause of our happiness; we sing for joy at the works of Your hands. **You supply the proper amounts of rain and snow to bring forth the harvest.** As the seed produces fruit, so Your Word produces fruit in the lives of Your people. **For the assurance of Your steadfast love, we give You thanks.**

As we grow toward maturity, we increasingly become aware that our days on earth are numbered. **As we anticipate the sound of the last trumpet, we know that, according to Your Word, we will all be changed.** As we contemplate that in a moment, in the twinkling of an eye, we shall be changed from our perishable nature to the imperishable, from mortality to immortality, our minds spin from such a mystery. **However, the assurance of Your Word helps us to look forward to our day of departure in hope, without fear.** For giving us the victory over death and the grave through our Lord Jesus Christ, **we give You humble and hearty thanks.**

Send us Your Holy Spirit that He may enlighten us to produce good fruit. **Help us to correct our own faults before we criticize others.** Cleanse our hearts that our mouths may speak good things. **Bless our government with capable and honest leaders.** May Your Church thrive under the leadership of consecrated Christians. **Grant peace to the warring nations of the world.**

(*Here special intercessions, silent or spoken, may be made. If spoken, each portion concludes:* Lord, in Your mercy, **hear our prayer.**)

Extend Your presence to the sick, the lonely, and the discouraged. **This we ask in the name of Jesus Christ, our Lord. Amen**

THE TRANSFIGURATION OF OUR LORD
Last Sunday after the Epiphany

Lord of glory, almighty King of the universe, and Lord of the Church, we praise You for establishing justice on the earth, and we extol Your holy name. **As we recognize Your leadership of the human race, we stand in awe before Your presence.** For the sake of Him whom You glorified on the holy mountain, we dare appear before You, trusting You to hear our prayer.

As through Your Word we behold the dazzling white clothing of Your glorified Son, we realize that our righteousness is like filthy rags. For being part of an adulterous generation that always looks for signs and wonders, forgive us, O Lord. **For not always being satisfied with the wonderful revelation of Your Word, forgive us, O Lord.**

Send us Your Holy Spirit, O Lord, that He may help us believe those truths we cannot understand. **Help us believe that the transfiguration glory may be ours one day when we assemble before Your throne with Jesus, Moses, and Elijah.** As You prepared Your Son for the cross by this magnificent manifestation of Your glory, so prepare us in the approaching Lenten season. **May we and the rest of the world find the solution to our individual, national, and international problems in the cross of Jesus Christ.**

(*Here special intercessions, silent or spoken, may be made. If spoken, each portion concludes:* Lord, in Your mercy, **hear our prayer.**)

Extend Your healing hand to the sick, lift up the depressed, and strengthen the weak. **We pray in the name of Jesus Christ, our Lord and Savior. Amen**

ASH WEDNESDAY

O God, Father of our Lord Jesus Christ and also our dear Father, **we thank You for permitting us to begin another Lenten season.** We are again privileged to meditate upon the cross of Christ and its meaning for us. **You have graciously granted us another opportunity for our relationship to be strengthened with Him who died to save us from our sins.** For Your gracious love, which prompted You to punish Your Son for our sins, **we give You humble and hearty thanks.**

In spirit we appear before You in sackcloth and ashes. **Send us Your Holy Spirit that He may help us to be genuinely sorry for our sins.** Help us to withstand the temptations of permitting the pleasures of this life, the worries of the day, and the activities of our daily routine to interfere with our Lenten worship and observance. **Draw us to Your wounded side and bring healing to our souls.** Help us to be conquerors over every temptation that confronts us.

(*Here special intercessions, silent or spoken, may be made. If spoken, each portion concludes:* Lord, in Your mercy, **hear our prayer.**)

Grant to Your Church an awareness of its responsibility to bring the Good News to everyone in the community. **Graciously bestow on us Your Holy Spirit so we may bear witness to You as our Savior.** To this end bless our Lenten services. **Grant us faithful attendance, and open our eyes to the opportunities for bringing others.** Add Your blessing to the Lenten messages, and through them strengthen our faith in Jesus Christ as our Savior. **This we ask in Jesus' name. Amen**

FIRST SUNDAY IN LENT

O Lord God Most High, almighty Fortress and Protector, we praise You for Your providence which has brought us to this hour. **In the midst of many dangers and temptations, we are still Your children by Your grace through faith in Jesus Christ.** Trusting in Your grace and mercy and believing Your promises to hear our prayers, we come before You with praise and thanksgiving.

We give You special thanks, O Lord, for sending Your Son into the world to become true man. Thank You that when He was tempted, as we are, He did not yield to sin but remained obedient to You for our sake. **When Satan tempts us through our fleshly appetites, the riches of this world, and our love for honor and prestige, help us to use Your Word as our weapon against him.** For inspiring men to write it, translate it, and print it so that it is readily available to us, we give You hearty thanks.

We confess, O Lord, that we often live as if bread for our bodies is more important than food for our souls. We confess, O Lord, that we often forget to use Your Word as the source of our strength in fighting temptation. **For these and many other transgressions, forgive us, O Lord.**

As we read, study, and hear Your Word, send us Your Holy Spirit to enlighten our minds and strengthen our faith. **May Your Word prove to be a power of healing to the sick, a ray of hope to the discouraged, and a companion to the lonely.**

(*Here special intercessions, silent or spoken, may be made. If spoken, each portion concludes:* Lord, in Your mercy, **hear our prayer.**)

Grant peace to our nation, and help us to live according to Your will. **In Jesus' name we pray. Amen**

SECOND SUNDAY IN LENT

Lord God, heavenly Father, we join our hearts in worship and praise. **The study of Your Word reveals more and more of Your love for us.** Even though Your prophets were persecuted and even killed, You sent Your Son to be our Prophet, Priest, and King. **For that love which would not be discouraged by man's inhumanity we give You honor, praise, and thanks.**

We confess that we have often been apathetic and indifferent towards Your message, spoken through Your prophets. **We have often failed to put Your Word into action.** In our failure to imitate the zeal, devotion, and love of our Savior, we may have turned many away from listening to Your message of salvation. **By being poor examples, we may have closed the channel of communication between them and ourselves.** For these and other sins, forgive us, O Lord.

Help us, O Lord, to be doers of Your Word and not hearers only. Help us to risk the enmity of others to proclaim and live Your truth. **Help us to conquer our enemies by increased zeal in spreading Your Gospel.** Help us, O Lord, to protect the falsely accused, to be companions to the lonely, and a source of hope to the discouraged. **Help us to be messengers of salvation to the straying and the lost.** Grant us peace in our time, O Lord, and peace to the other nations of this world.

(*Here special intercessions, silent or spoken, may be made. If spoken, each portion concludes:* Lord, in Your mercy, **hear our prayer.**)

Grant these, our petitions, according to Your will. **We pray in the name of and for the sake of Jesus Christ, our Lord and Savior. Amen**

THIRD SUNDAY IN LENT

O Lord God Eternal, the God of Abraham, Isaac, and Jacob, we praise You for the great things You have done for Your chosen people. **When they were suffering in slavery under the Egyptians, Your hand was mighty to deliver them.** Through Your special agent, Moses, You brought Your people from tyranny and oppression to a land flowing with milk and honey. **For making the New Testament Church Your chosen people through Christ and for making us part of it, we give You thanks.**

We confess that we have not always lived up to our high calling in Christ. **We confess that we have often been unproductive fig trees in Your vineyard.** We confess that we have often passed judgment on others rather than showing mercy. **For our failures and sins, O Lord, forgive us.**

Send us Your Holy Spirit, O Lord, to give us wisdom and understanding about Your dealings with people. **Enlighten our minds that we may recognize Your will.** Strengthen us, O Lord, that we may also do Your will.

Grant stability to our government and peace to our world. Extend Your hand of healing to the sick and grant sustenance to the poverty-stricken. **Comfort the bereaved with the hope of the great resurrection, and assure the lonely of Your presence.**

(*Here special intercessions, silent or spoken, may be made. If spoken, each portion concludes:* Lord, in Your mercy, **hear our prayer.**)

In the name of Him who suffered and died for us, **our Lord and Savior, Jesus Christ. Amen**

FOURTH SUNDAY IN LENT

Lord God, heavenly Father, we are thankful that with You we have forgiveness. **How blessed we are that for the sake of Your Son, You do not hold us guilty for our iniquities.** Although You have just reasons to be angry with us for our sins, we are thankful that Your Son's sacrifice has turned Your anger away from us. **We no longer need to be afraid of Your justice; we trust in Your mercy.** You have turned our weakness into strength for the sake of Your Son, our Savior, Jesus Christ.

Having already received our inheritance in the certainty of our salvation, help us to let others know that they may have the same inheritance. Make us realize that by sharing this inheritance, we increase our joy as well as theirs. **Do not permit us to envy those to whom You seemingly have given more and greater blessings.** Help us to welcome into our fellowship all who receive Your Son as their Savior.

Be with our own nation and the nations of the world. Bring to naught the threats of war so that the rumors of war may be dispelled. **Grant that the peace established between previously warring nations may be a lasting one.** Be with the refugees of war-torn countries, and help them find in You their strength and sustenance. **Increase our zeal in spreading the Gospel of Jesus Christ, which alone can bring lasting peace to the world.** May the sick find in You their healing strength. **Lead the erring back to Your fold, and help us to live to Your honor and glory.**

(*Here special intercessions, silent or spoken, may be made. If spoken, each portion concludes:* Lord, in Your mercy, **hear our prayer.**)

Bless our nation with peace, and help us to live in harmony with Your will. **We pray in the name of Jesus Christ, our Savior. Amen**

FIFTH SUNDAY IN LENT

Father of our Lord Jesus Christ and our Father, we come before You with praise and thanksgiving. **We praise You for having heard our prayers and supplications.** We thank You for being our strength and shield. **Because You have not been deaf to our cries, nor silent to our voices, we again lift up our hands of supplication in confidence and trust.** We believe that You will hear us.

We know, O Lord, that we are far from being perfect. Yet we press on toward the goal for the prize of Your upward call in Christ Jesus. **The path of our life here on earth is covered with many failures and sins.** Therefore we do not appear before You in our own righteousness. **We come before You with faith in the righteousness of Jesus Christ, our Lord.** According to Your promise, forgive us, O Lord. **Assured of Your forgiveness through Your Son, O Lord, help us to forget the sins and failures of the past.** Give us renewed courage and strength to face the future. **Trusting in Your Word and promise, we walk into the future unafraid, for we know You will be with us.**

(*Here special intercessions, silent or spoken, may be made. If spoken, each portion concludes:* Lord, in Your mercy, **hear our prayer.**)

O Lord, we look forward to the day when all believers in Christ can share the joy of His resurrection to life everlasting. **May Your Holy Spirit keep us and all our loved ones in the faith until You call us from earth to heaven.**

We commend to You our nation and all those who are in positions of leadership in church and state. **Hear us for Jesus' sake. Amen**

PALM SUNDAY
Sunday of the Passion

With hosannas we come before You, O Lord of hosts. **We praise You for sending us Your Son as the King who came in Your name to establish peace between heaven and earth.** We are thankful that He did not consider Himself too far above us to become true man. **We deeply appreciate His fulfillment of the Law, which we are unable to keep.** We cannot adequately express our thanks that Christ took our punishment upon Himself by dying on the cross.

O Lord Jesus Christ, this day we confess that we have not always been faithful to our calling as Your chosen people. The deeds of our lives have often not matched the confession of our lips. **We have often broken communications with You by neglecting prayer, by failing to study Your Word, and by failing to partake regularly of Your sacraments.**

Because we know, O Lord, that You are merciful, we dare to come before You, begging forgiveness. **May the assurance of that forgiveness, which we receive through Your Word and sacraments, enable us to live lives of dedicated discipleship.**

Send us Your Holy Spirit to keep us on the path that leads to You. **Help us to withstand the temptations of Satan, the world, and our flesh.** Grant us grace to live to Your honor and glory **so that our lives will reflect our eternal gratitude for the salvation You won for us through Your life of perfect obedience and through Your sacrificial suffering and death.**

(*Here special intercessions, silent or spoken, may be made. If spoken, each portion concludes:* Lord, in Your mercy, **hear our prayer.**)

May Your kingdom reach into the lives of the sick, the disabled, and the lonely. **This we ask in the name of the King of kings, Jesus Christ, our Lord. Amen**

MAUNDY THURSDAY

Lord God, heavenly Father, Author of the everlasting covenant and Giver of the cup of salvation, we Your children, gather in Your courts to offer You our sacrifice of thanksgiving. **For fulfilling Your promise to establish a new covenant through the blood of Your Son Jesus Christ, we give You humble and hearty thanks.** Through the veil of His flesh we enter the Holy of Holies of Your presence without fear or trembling. **As our Lord Jesus Christ gave thanks to You when He broke the bread,** as He gave thanks to You when He took the cup, so we give You thanks.

Lord Jesus Christ, both our High Priest and the offering, awe and wonder fill our hearts as we partake of Your body, broken for us, and Your blood, shed for us. In our poverty of righteousness we have nothing to offer but our sins and gratitude. **Without Your tremendous sacrifice we would still be in our sins.** But thanks be to You, for through Your Sacrament of the New Testament we are assured that our iniquities are forgiven and our sins are no longer remembered.

O Holy Spirit, dwell within us as we remember in this Sacrament our Lord's death. Enter our hearts and help us show our gratitude by encouraging one another to love and good works. **As our Lord served His disciples by washing their feet, so may we also humbly serve one another.**

(*Here special intercessions, silent or spoken, may be made. If spoken, each portion concludes:* Lord, in Your mercy, **hear our prayer.**)

Help us to live our lives as sacrifices of thanksgiving to Him who first loved us. **In His name we pray. Amen**

GOOD FRIDAY

Lord God, heavenly Father, this day marks the anniversary of Your greatest gift to the world. **Your love for the human race is beyond our understanding.** We praise You for that love, which caused You to give up Your only-begotten Son unto death for sinful humanity. **Cleansed of our sin and clothed in His righteousness, we can now stand in Your presence.** We thank You for making us the beneficiaries of Your love in Christ.

O Lord Jesus Christ, we will never know the full extent of Your suffering for us. Because You asked Your Father to forgive those who put You on the cross, we know that our sins have also been forgiven. **Because You promised the criminal who believed in You everlasting life,** we have the assurance that, in spite of our sins, we too may have eternal life. **As in the midst of Your suffering You had consideration for Your mother,** we can be confident You will be with us to the end of our earthly life. **Because You were forsaken by God the Father,** we know that we shall never be forsaken. **Because You thirsted for us,** we now have the water of everlasting life. **Because of Your declaration that the work of redemption was finished,** we no longer need to be doubtful about our salvation. **Through Your yielding up Your spirit to death,** we have life.

O Holy Spirit, abide in our hearts. Help us to believe that Christ died in our place. **Grant us a faith that bears testimony to our friends and community that this salvation is also available to them.**

(Here special intercessions, silent or spoken, may be made. If spoken, each portion concludes: Lord, in Your mercy, **hear our prayer.**)

So fill us with Your Holy Spirit that our lives will be a constant witness to our faith in the crucified Christ. **This we ask in the name of Jesus Christ, our Lord and Savior. Amen**

THE RESURRECTION OF OUR LORD
Easter Day

O God of life and Father of our Lord Jesus Christ, according to Your abundant grace, You have begotten us again to a new and living hope by the resurrection of Jesus from the dead. **You have transformed the night of doubt and sorrow into the new and eternal day of joy and gladness.** You have brought life and immortality to light by the glad tidings that Christ is risen. **For this, O Lord, we give You thanks.** You have delivered Your Son, who died for our sins, from the grip of death and raised Him by Your power. **That which You sowed in dishonor and weakness, You raised in power and glory.** O Lord, we praise You that through Him You removed death's sting for us. **You have brought us victory over the grave.**

Fill our hearts with the joy of the resurrection. **Grant to Your Church and people everywhere the power of the resurrected Christ.** Help us to show forth Your praises. **Bless our homes with the comfort and hope of Easter.** Send the conquering banner of Christ's victory into all the world. **Grant that many more nations may join the hosts of heaven in songs of triumph.**

In the promise of Easter take away from us all fear of death. **Let the radiant beams of Easter's light shine into the depths of our souls.** Renew us in the Spirit of Him who is the Way, the Truth, and the Life. **Speak peace to our souls and maintain our faith in Him who promises resurrection and life.**

(*Here special intercessions, silent or spoken, may be made. If spoken, each portion concludes:* Lord, in Your mercy, **hear our prayer.**)

Visit with Your presence those who are sick, lonely, and discouraged. **We pray in the name of our risen Lord. Amen**

SECOND SUNDAY OF EASTER

Lord God, heavenly Father, the earthshaking news of Your Son's resurrection gives us a new song to sing. **We, the children of Zion, rejoice in our resurrected King.** By His resurrection You have assured us of His victory over death and hell. **Every minute of every day of our lives is not sufficient time in which to give You adequate thanks.**

We confess that our lives do not always reflect the assurance and joy You have given us through Your Son's resurrection. **Too often we have been doubting Thomases, looking for tangible evidence.** Too often we have failed to let others know that we believe Jesus Christ is Your Son and the living victorious Savior of the world. **Help us accept the witness of Your disciples in Your Word.**

For our many moments of doubt, forgive us, O Lord. **For looking for signs instead of searching Your Word, forgive us, O Lord.**

O Lord Jesus Christ, as You gave Your peace to Your disciples, so may that peace abide with us. As You gave Philip the mission to tell the man in the chariot about You, so lead us to someone who needs to know You as Savior.

O Holy Spirit of the living God, make Your presence felt in our nation and in the churches. May Your Church hold high the lighted candle of the Gospel. **Add Your blessings to our efforts and turn the hearts of many to follow Christ.**

(*Here special intercessions, silent or spoken, may be made. If spoken, each portion concludes:* Lord, in Your mercy, **hear our prayer.**)

Bless our nation with peace, and help us to live in harmony with Your will. **In Jesus' name we pray. Amen**

THIRD SUNDAY OF EASTER

O Lord God Most High, we would give You thanks forever. **In a moment of this world's history You showed Your anger at its sin and corruption by laying its guilt on Your Son.** You caused Him to suffer at the hands of sinful men. **For a moment—because of our guilt—You withheld Your presence from Him.** And finally You let Him die in our place.

But wonder of wonders, You did not let Him remain in death, but for our sake You gloriously raised Him to life. Now we know that He accomplished every detail of Your most holy will. **He fulfilled all righteousness for us and has turned our weeping into joy.**

And yet, O Lord, we must confess that we often lack a confident faith in His resurrection because He has not appeared to us personally. **Our mortality crowds in on us, and we often long for a greater measure of His presence.** We would love to have Him eat breakfast with us as He did with Peter and John. **For this weakness of faith, we ask Your forgiveness.**

Help us realize that the spread of Christ's kingdom throughout the world is evidence that He is Your Son and our Savior. **As the first disciples risked their lives to obey You rather than man, help us to show a similar courage.** If we are called to suffer for our faith, may we also rejoice in being worthy to suffer.

(*Here special intercessions, silent or spoken, may be made. If spoken, each portion concludes:* Lord, in Your mercy, **hear our prayer.**)

For those who are suffering, we ask Your divine strength. **In Jesus' name we pray. Amen**

FOURTH SUNDAY OF EASTER

Dear heavenly Father, as we continue to celebrate the resurrection of Your Son Jesus Christ, we praise You for giving us this solid foundation on which to build Your Church. **We praise You for the witnesses who were willing to sacrifice their lives in defense of the resurrection truth.** We praise You for opening the doors of Your kingdom to us Gentiles so that we also may be part of Your flock. **We thank You for the apostles, who risked their lives to proclaim the message of Christ's resurrection to the world.**

We confess that our witness to our risen Lord often falls short of the courage evidenced by the early Christians. **We confess that our sacrifices are trivial compared to those who gave their lives as witnesses to the resurrection truth.** We confess that we have not always reflected the resurrection joy to our families, fellow workers, and community. **We confess that we should be more zealous in inviting outsiders into Your kingdom.** We confess that we have been timid when we should have been courageous and bold when we should have been meek. **For our errors in judgment and other transgressions, forgive us, O Lord.**

Help us to fear no evil when we and our loved ones walk through the valley of the shadow of death. **Lead us beside the still waters so that our souls may be restored.** Use us to bring all people into Your one fold, where, according to Your promise, we may have eternal life now and forevermore.

(*Here special intercessions, silent or spoken, may be made. If spoken, each portion concludes:* Lord, in Your mercy, **hear our prayer.**)

We commend to Your care all those whose special needs require the assurance of Your presence. **In Jesus' name. Amen**

FIFTH SUNDAY OF EASTER

Almighty, everlasting God, Father of our Lord Jesus Christ, gracious and merciful, slow to anger, and abounding in steadfast love, accept our praise for mightily delivering us from the punishment of our sins. **We praise You especially for having brought us, who were outside the boundaries of Your chosen people, to the knowledge of salvation.** We are unworthy of Your consideration.

O Lord, we confess that in spite of Your patience with us, we have been impatient with those who still reject You. We have often failed to demonstrate Christian love even toward those who have faith in You. **We have often broken our Lord's commandment to love one another.**

For our lack of patience and our lovelessness, forgive us, O Lord. **As members of Christ's body, as a Church founded on the certainty of His resurrection, we have often failed to show the world that we are governed by Your love.** Forgive us, O Lord.

Send us Your Holy Spirit that we may be perfected in love. Help us to be more patient with one another and with the world we are trying to win. **Help us to be faithful to our Lord and Savior Jesus Christ that the world may recognize us as His disciples.** Strengthen our faith in Your promise of a new heaven and a new earth, where You will wipe away every tear from our eyes, replace our sorrow with joy, and make an eternal home for us.

(*Here special intercessions, silent or spoken, may be made. If spoken, each portion concludes:* Lord, in Your mercy, **hear our prayer.**)

For those who need Your special care, **we pray in Jesus' name. Amen**

SIXTH SUNDAY OF EASTER

Dear heavenly Father, as Your children by grace through faith in our resurrected Lord, Jesus Christ, we come before You in praise and adoration. **We praise You for guiding the founders of Your Church.** Through the Holy Spirit You led them in the way of truth, enabling them to proclaim Your Gospel with certainty and conviction.

We confess that we have not always proclaimed Your Gospel with the same certainty. We confess that we have often confused those who would be followers of Christ with traditions and practices that are not essential to their salvation. **We confess that we have frequently urged the observance of human ordinances as conditions for discipleship.** We confess that our zeal has often clouded our sense of good judgment in matters requiring divine knowledge. **For these and other transgressions that have hindered the growth of Your kingdom on earth, forgive us, O Lord.**

O Lord Jesus Christ, we ask for Your peace. **Calm our troubled minds and hearts with that peace which the world cannot give.** While humanity longs for the absence of war and conflict, grant peace among the many divisions of Christianity today, that from Your Church the world may learn of Your peace. **Give us patience to listen that we may understand one another better.** Send us Your Holy Spirit that He may help us to determine Your truth and live according to it. **May Your love govern the council of nations, and may justice and righteousness prevail in our own land.**

(*Here special intercessions, silent or spoken, may be made. If spoken, each portion concludes:* Lord, in Your mercy, **hear our prayer.**)

Help us reach that Holy City where Your glory shines forever more. **Hear us for Jesus' sake. Amen**

THE ASCENSION OF OUR LORD

O Lord Jesus Christ, exalted far above all principalities, power, might, and dominion, at whose name every knee should bow, not only in this world but also in the world to come, **accept our praise and adoration.**

We know that our praise cannot exalt You any higher than the position You already have at the right hand of God the Father, **yet we are bold enough to believe that You delight in the commendation of Your children.** Accept our humble thanks for giving us the privilege of being part of Your body, the Church.

For the many appearances You made after Your resurrection, proving to witnesses that You had risen from the dead, we are grateful. We also thank You for assembling so many of the faithful to witness Your ascension. **These witnesses to Your resurrection and ascension inspire us to follow You.**

As the ascended Head of the Church, O Lord, You are aware of the many problems confronting the Church today. **We do not ask that our work be made easier, but only for Your power to help us cope with the problems.** Help us to be Your hands, doing deeds of kindness. **Help us to be Your feet, running errands of mercy.** Help us to be Your mouth, witnessing to Your love and salvation.

(*Here special intercessions, silent or spoken, may be made. If spoken, each portion concludes:* Lord, in Your mercy, **hear our prayer.**)

When at last we have fulfilled Your purpose in our lives, **take us to Your ascension throne, where we may share Your glory forevermore. Amen**

SEVENTH SUNDAY OF EASTER

O Lord God, King of all the earth, we praise You for Your creation of the universe and for making us the crown of Your creation. **O Lord Jesus Christ, we thank You for becoming our Paschal Lamb and paying the penalty for our sins with Your blood.** O Holy Spirit, we adore You for calling us to faith in Jesus Christ as our Savior and for preserving us in that faith. **O Father, Son, and Holy Spirit, for Your creation, redemption, and sanctification, accept our humble thanks.**

For such dedicated men as Paul and Timothy, who were obedient to Your call when the assigned mission differed with their own judgment, **we give You thanks.**

We confess, O Lord, that we have often acted as ungrateful children. **We have often followed our own way rather than submitting to Yours.** We have wasted the resources of Your creation. **We have failed to proclaim the joy of Christ's resurrection and His exaltation to Your right hand.** We have not made full use of Your means of grace. **We have inadvertently been the cause of discord when we were trying to create harmony.** We have disrupted the unity of Your Church by being divisive, and that often for non-Scriptural reasons.

Help us, O Lord, to remember that You desire Your believers to exhibit their faith in unity. May the world recognize in us the love that You shared with Your Son Jesus Christ. **Give us the courage to testify for Your truth without fear of consequences.** Inspire the fainthearted, be a source of hope to the discouraged, and assure the lonely of Your presence.

(*Here special intercessions, silent or spoken, may be made. If spoken, each portion concludes:* Lord, in Your mercy, **hear our prayer.**)

In the midst of trials and temptations, **come quickly, Lord. Amen**

PENTECOST

Lord God, heavenly Father, who together with Your Son and the Holy Spirit created the universe and every living being, we, Your creatures, praise You for Your mighty works. **We thank You for sending Your Son, who died as a righteous man for our unrighteousness.** Accept the gratefulness of our hearts for also sending Your Holy Spirit. **He has created in us the faith to believe that Your Son is our Savior.** We sing Your praises for His visitation and for Christ's resurrection and ascension.

On this anniversary of the founding of Your Church on earth, we thank You for revealing to us the power of Your Holy Spirit. As You once manifested Your power by curbing man's ambition at the tower of Babel with a confusion of tongues, **we praise You that on Pentecost You enabled everyone to hear in his own language about Your mighty works.**

O Lord, we have seen Your wonders in the heavens and have witnessed Your power on earth. **In spite of the revelation of Your glory we often go our own way, ignoring Your presence.** Our indifference is exceeded only by those who do not know You and have not experienced the gift of faith by Your Holy Spirit.

(Here special intercessions, silent or spoken, may be made. If spoken, each portion concludes: Lord, in Your mercy, **hear our prayer.**)

Pour out Your Holy Spirit upon us, O Lord, that He may help us persevere in the faith. **In Jesus' name we pray. Amen**

THE HOLY TRINITY
First Sunday after Pentecost

God the Father, God the Son, and God the Holy Spirit, One in Three and Three in One, **accept our praise for our creation, redemption, and sanctification.**

O Father, Author of our creation, how majestic is Your name in all the earth. **The moon and stars, the works of Your fingers, reflect Your glory.** When man, the crown of Your creation, failed to reflect Your glory, You visited him in the form of Your Son Jesus Christ. **We are indeed thankful that Your image, which man lost, may be restored through faith in the suffering, death, resurrection, and ascension of Your willing servant, Jesus.**

O Lord Jesus Christ, we humbly bring You our praises. **For leaving the throne of Your glory, we give You thanks.** For dwelling among us as true man, we give You thanks. **For being tempted as we are, we are thankful.** For taking upon Yourself our sins and accepting the punishment for them, we give You thanks. **For justifying us before the Father, we give You thanks.** We confess that we have repaid You miserably for this gift of salvation. **For Your loving-kindness we have repaid You with lovelessness.** For Your love and zeal in working out our salvation we have repaid You with apathy and indifference. **For these our miserable offenses forgive us, O Lord.**

O Holy Spirit, enter our hearts, we pray. **Help us to endure tribulation with patience.** Fill our hearts with hope. **Help us to accept the forgiveness earned for us by Christ. Grant us Your peace.**

(*Here special intercessions, silent or spoken, may be made. If spoken, each portion concludes:* Lord, in Your mercy, **hear our prayer.**)

O Father, Son, and Holy Spirit, ever One in Three and Three in One, accept the praise we bring from grateful hearts. **In Jesus' name we pray. Amen**

SECOND SUNDAY AFTER PENTECOST

Lord God, heavenly Father, God of mercy and God of truth, we come before You as Your children in Christ Jesus, our Savior. **With no righteousness of our own, we stand before You in the righteousness of Your Son.** Accept our praise for Your mercy and for Your truth, which endure forever.

We confess, O Lord, that we have often been more concerned about ourselves than about the strangers in Your gates. We confess that we are often more concerned with pleasing people than with pleasing You. **We confess that we pray more for ourselves than for others.** We have often failed to bear witness to the Gospel by the way we live. **For these and other sins, which You know only too well, forgive us, O Lord.**

Send us Your Holy Spirit that He may guide us into all truth. **Renew our faith in Your power to heal.** We implore Your healing power upon those who are dear to us and of the household of faith. **Extend Your healing power also to those who are strangers to us and do not know You as their Savior.** Through the evidence of Your power may they recognize You as the only true God and Jesus Christ, whom You have sent. **As You healed the centurion's servant, so extend Your healing hand on those for whom we now pray.**

(Here special intercessions, silent or spoken, may be made. If spoken, each portion concludes: Lord, in Your mercy, **hear our prayer.**)

O Holy Spirit, visit us and those who receive the healing of our Lord Jesus Christ with a faith that saves not only their bodies but their souls as well. **May we ever gratefully remember to glorify You as You answer our calls in the day of trouble.** Grant these our petitions **in the name of our Great Physician, Jesus Christ, our Lord. Amen**

THIRD SUNDAY AFTER PENTECOST

O Lord our God, Source of all life, we, Your creatures, come before You in worship and praise. **For the breath of life, which sustains us each hour, we give You thanks.** For the joys and pleasures that come to us through Your creation, we give You thanks. **But especially for the promise of eternal life through Your Son Jesus Christ, we give thanks to You forever.**

We confess that we have not always respected the gift of life that comes from Your almighty hand. **We confess that we have not been sufficiently concerned about improving the quality of life for others.** We have often abused the gift of life in the pursuit of selfish interests. **We have not been zealous enough to increase the quality of our own lives.** We confess that we have failed in our duty and privilege of bringing to others the knowledge of eternal life through Christ. **For these and countless other transgressions against Your laws of life, forgive us, O Lord.**

Help us, O Lord, to increase the usefulness of our lives in Your service and in service to others. **Help us to answer the needs of others less fortunate than we, that they too may more fully enjoy life.** Preserve the form of government in our nation so that we may continue to enjoy our lives in freedom.

(*Here special intercessions, silent or spoken, may be made. If spoken, each portion concludes:* Lord, in Your mercy, **hear our prayer.**)

Help us to use wisely the time of earthly life allotted to us. **Keep us steadfast in the faith so that we can face the end of our life on earth with courage, not fear.** Help us believe in Your promise of eternal life through Your Son Jesus Christ. **In His name we pray. Amen**

FOURTH SUNDAY AFTER PENTECOST

Lord God, heavenly Father, God of justice, mercy, and forgiveness, we come before You with thankful hearts. **We adore You for sending us Your Son Jesus Christ, who satisfied Your justice by taking upon Himself the punishment of our sins.** We stand before You justified, not by our works of the Law, but by faith in Jesus Christ.

Once again we appeal to Your mercy and spirit of forgiveness. Like Your servant David, we have often used others to attain for ourselves unworthy goals. **In our efforts to appear righteous, we have allowed others to take the blame for our transgressions.** We have often insisted that others keep the Law, while we ourselves have compromised with evil. **We have often judged others as greater sinners than ourselves.** You have forgiven us much, yet we have been reluctant to forgive others. **For these and all our offenses against Your love, forgive us, O Lord.**

Guard us from the temptation to sin when others may not be aware of our sin. **Strengthen us to live our private lives as well as our public lives as in Your presence.** Bless us with honest and upright officials in government. **Give us dedicated and consecrated leadership in the administration of the church's affairs.**

May Your Holy Spirit give vision to the shortsighted and a knowledge of Your presence to the lonely. **Grant hope for healing to the sick, and a goal for living to the discouraged.**

(*Here special intercessions, silent or spoken, may be made. If spoken, each portion concludes:* Lord, in Your mercy, **hear our prayer.**)

Help us to rejoice in Your mercy. **In Jesus' name we pray. Amen**

FIFTH SUNDAY AFTER PENTECOST

Dear heavenly Father, we, Your children, who have been baptized into Your family by faith in Jesus Christ, come to You. **Accept our praise for choosing us to be adopted into Your family so that we may become heirs to Your promise of salvation.**

As Your children, we confess that we have not always behaved as children of a kind heavenly Father. **We have often disrupted that peace You expect from those who are united by faith in Your Son Jesus Christ.** We confess that we have often discriminated against other members of Your family who are from different ethnic backgrounds. **We confess that we fail consistently to acknowledge Your Son as the Christ whom You have sent.** We have tried to follow Him without self-denial, and we have borne our crosses too unwillingly. **We have lived selfishly and have been reluctant to lose any part of our life in His service.** For these and all our transgressions, forgive us, O heavenly Father.

Send us Your Holy Spirit that He may strengthen our faith in Your beloved Son Jesus Christ. Help us to be bold in our witness to Him as the Christ whom You have sent. **Strengthen our spiritual feet that we may walk more firmly in His footsteps.** Help our government to administer the affairs of state according to Your will. **Bless Your Church with the spirit of mercy and sacrifice.** Cheer the sick and lonely with the assurance of Your presence.

(*Here special intercessions, silent or spoken, may be made. If spoken, each portion concludes:* Lord, in Your mercy, **hear our prayer.**)

Grant peace to all nations that Your Word may spread unhampered throughout the world. **This we ask in the name of and for the sake of Jesus, our Lord. Amen**

SIXTH SUNDAY AFTER PENTECOST

O holy heavenly Father, we give You thanks for providing us a goodly heritage through our Lord Jesus Christ. **Our hearts are glad, and our souls rejoice in Your promise that in Your presence there is fullness of joy and at Your right hand there are pleasures forevermore.**

We confess that we become discouraged when we consider how many there are who fail to recognize Your power and mercy. **We often forget that there are many who honor You through receiving Your Son Jesus Christ as their Savior.** We confess that we are often led into temptations by our flesh, rather than permitting Your Holy Spirit to guide us. **We have often used our Christian freedom as a license to do those things which displease You and give offense to others.** We confess that we have often failed to witness to the suffering, death, and resurrection of Jesus Christ for fear that such knowledge might be unacceptable to them. **For these and many other sins against Your holy will, we ask Your forgiveness.**

Help us walk in the Spirit and withstand the temptation to follow the inclinations of our flesh. **Send us Your Holy Spirit that He may teach us to follow Christ and produce the fruits of the Spirit.** Instill in us a desire for love and joy, peace and patience, kindness and goodness, gentleness, and self-control.

(*Here special intercessions, silent or spoken, may be made. If spoken, each portion concludes:* Lord, in Your mercy, **hear our prayer.**)

Give us the faith to follow our Lord Jesus Christ even in the face of suffering and sacrifice. **All this we ask in His name. Amen**

SEVENTH SUNDAY AFTER PENTECOST

With joy in our hearts and the voice of thanksgiving on our lips, we praise Your glorious name, O Lord. **Accept our thanks for keeping us among the living and for keeping watch over the nations.** We implore You to listen to the voice of our prayers as we come to You in the name of Your Son Jesus Christ.

As we hear Your Word, we realize how negligent we have been. We have been aware of erring brethren but have not attempted to correct them in the spirit of kindness. **We have been aware of other people's burdens but have kept ourselves from getting involved.** We have held ourselves in high esteem and depreciated the efforts of others. **We have sown to the flesh, expecting to reap from the spirit.** We are aware of the plentiful harvest of souls and the lack of workers, yet we continue to stand idle. **For our many sins of commission and omission, forgive us, O Lord.**

Send us Your Holy Spirit that the cross of Christ might be for us a new creation. **Help us not to grow weary in welldoing.** Strengthen us to do good to all, especially to those who are of the household of faith. **Grant healing to the sick, comfort to the lonely, encouragement to the disheartened, and joy to the sorrowing.**

(*Here special intercessions, silent or spoken, may be made. If spoken, each portion concludes:* Lord, in Your mercy, **hear our prayer.**)

Bless the president of our nation with wisdom and understanding; our congress, with dedication to serve all the people; and our nation, with peace. **Not because of any merit on our part, but for Your mercy's sake, we pray in Jesus' name. Amen**

EIGHTH SUNDAY AFTER PENTECOST

We lift up our souls to You, O Lord, in whom we trust. **Mindful of Your mercy and Your steadfast truth, accept our adoration and praise.** Surrounded by humanity's injustice and untruthfulness, it is refreshing to know and believe that You are the Source for all truth and mercy. **We thank You for the truth, revealed in Your Word, that our salvation is in Jesus Christ, Your Son.** We thank You for Your undeserved love, which prompted You to send us salvation through the person of Your Son Jesus Christ.

As recipients of Your gracious love, we regret that we have failed to show You adequate thanks. We have not loved You with all our heart, soul, strength, and mind. **As a result, we have also not loved our neighbor as ourselves.** Aware of those who need our help, we, like the priest and the Levite, have often passed by on the other side. **Not only have we neglected to meet our neighbor's physical needs, but we have also failed to supply his spiritual needs.** For our lack of zeal in sharing our earthly gifts and the gift of salvation, forgive us, O Lord.

Help us to be strengthened with all power according to Your glorious might that we may bear fruit in every good work and increase in divine knowledge. Give us that endurance which reveals itself in patience and joy as we work for the expansion of Your kingdom. **We pray for those who are in physical or spiritual need.**

(*Here special intercessions, silent or spoken, may be made. If spoken, each portion concludes:* Lord, in Your mercy, **hear our prayer.**)

Bless our nation with peace, and help us to remain in harmony with Your will. **In Jesus' name we pray. Amen**

NINTH SUNDAY AFTER PENTECOST

O Lord God, heavenly Father, with You as the Light of our salvation, **we have nothing to fear.** You are the Stronghold of our life, and therefore there is no one whom we need fear. **It is our joy to dwell in Your house and pray to You as we behold Your beauty in Your temple.** According to Your promise we know that, if we seek You, we will find You. **Give us the patience and courage to wait for You so that we may see Your goodness in the land of the living.**

We know, O Lord, that You desire us to walk blamelessly before You, but we cannot do so without Your help. **As You counted Abraham's faith for righteousness, so count our faith in Your Son Jesus Christ as righteousness.** In His righteousness we dare to stand before You and make our wishes known. **Of ourselves, we are not worthy of any of the things for which we ask.** We have not rejoiced in our sufferings, and we have tried to escape from suffering for You and for the sake of our neighbor. **We have not been zealous in teaching others the way of salvation.** We have busied ourselves with many earthly things and neglected many opportunities to sit at Your feet and hear Your Word. **We have been more eager to provide food for our bodies than to seek nourishment for our souls.** For this lack of spiritual awareness and neglect of Your truth, **forgive us, O Lord.**

(*Here special intercessions, silent or spoken, may be made. If spoken, each portion concludes:* Lord, in Your mercy, **hear our prayer.**)

Preserve religious freedom in our nation, and bless our world with peace that Your Church may flourish. **We pray in Jesus' name. Amen**

TENTH SUNDAY AFTER PENTECOST

We give thanks to You, O Lord, with our whole heart. **Because You have answered our prayers and delivered us from the midst of trouble, we know, O Lord, that Your steadfast love endures forever.** Therefore we are bold to come before You through the merits of Jesus Christ, Your Son, with these petitions.

We regret, O Lord, that in spite of Your loving-kindnesses we have often repaid You with our sins. Our sinful selves have been buried with Christ in Baptism, but we often fail to rise to newness of life. **You have given us ample assurance in Your Word that in Christ all our sins are forgiven, yet we often fail to accept this forgiveness with our whole heart.** You have assured us that when we ask, You will give, **when we seek, we shall find,** and when we knock, it shall be opened to us. **Yet we have prayed with less than wholehearted faith in Your promises.** You assure us again and again that You will give the Holy Spirit to those who ask, yet we fail to ask. **We have often abused the Lord's Prayer by saying it without thinking or doubting when we pray.** For these and all our transgressions, forgive us, O Lord.

Empower us with Your Holy Spirit. May He strengthen our faith in Your good providence. **Help us to pray with meaning, trusting that we have been redeemed through Christ.** Bless our leadership in church and state with wisdom, understanding, and dedication to service.

(*Here special intercessions, silent or spoken, may be made. If spoken, each portion concludes:* Lord, in Your mercy, **hear our prayer.**)

Be a source of help to the helpless and a source of hope to the hopeless. **In Jesus' name we pray. Amen**

ELEVENTH SUNDAY AFTER PENTECOST

Lord God, heavenly Father, You provide us with all things needful for sustaining our lives on earth. **You have also made provisions for the salvation of our souls in sending Your Son Jesus Christ.** Accept our praise and adoration for Your physical and spiritual providence.

Truly, O Lord, we do not deserve Your kindness, for we have sinned against You and are no more worthy to be called Your children. You have given us untold treasures on this earth, yet we are so busy collecting them that we often forget that they come from You. **We often forget that our accumulated wealth and possessions cannot redeem our souls.** We have often coveted earthly wealth to the neglect of Your Word and sacraments. **We have been selfish by not sharing our treasure with You and with others.** Because of the competition for earthly things, we have often become angry with our neighbor and been guilty of slander. **For these and all our transgressions against Your holy will, forgive us, O Lord.**

Breathe within us a spirit of contentment. **Having food and clothing, let us be content.** Give us faith to share with You the fruits of our labor. **Help us not to begrudge the good fortunes of others.** Increase our awareness of the needs of others, and use us to alleviate the pangs of hunger so prevalent in our world today.

(*Here special intercessions, silent or spoken, may be made. If spoken, each portion concludes:* Lord, in Your mercy, **hear our prayer.**)

Breathe a spirit of contentment into the council of nations, and grant all a spirit of generosity. **May there be peace on earth. We pray in Jesus' name. Amen**

TWELFTH SUNDAY AFTER PENTECOST

We rejoice, O Lord God Almighty, because You have made us righteous through the merits of Your Son Jesus Christ. **As Your mercies are new every morning so may we sing You each day a new song.** We adore You for the truth of Your Word, and praise You for Your righteousness and justice. **We appear before You in the righteousness of Jesus Christ and for His sake ask You to hear our prayer.**

Even though the holiness of Christ covers our sin, we know that we are still sinners. **We have had many more fulfillments of Your promises to encourage us to believe in You than did Abraham, and yet we have failed to follow Your guidance.** Frequently we have doubted the fulfillment of Your promises, even though Your promise of sending a Savior has been fulfilled. **We have concentrated too much on the material things of this life, forgetting that we are but pilgrims on this earth on our way to heaven.** We have been apathetic and lazy in working for Your kingdom, procrastinating because we have not believed our Lord's Second Coming is near. **In our pursuit of worldly pleasures we have not always remained alert to meet Your Son.** For our waywardness, O Lord, forgive us.

Recreate us and help us more fully to realize that we are heirs to heavenly riches that far exceed anything we may gather on this earth. Keep us alert and busy in Your kingdom that we may be ready to meet the Lord Jesus Christ when He comes.

(*Here special intercessions, silent or spoken, may be made. If spoken, each portion concludes:* Lord, in Your mercy, **hear our prayer.**)

Grant wisdom and understanding to those who govern us that they may do so for the benefit of all, and help us all to carry out Your Great Commission. **We pray in Jesus' name. Amen**

THIRTEENTH SUNDAY AFTER PENTECOST

Dear Father in heaven, we praise and adore You for Your unfailing presence both near and far. **We thank You for making Yourself available to us no matter where we may be.** It is comforting to know that we are never beyond the reach of Your mercy. **Therefore we have full assurance that You will hear us as we come before You in the name of our Lord Jesus Christ.**

While it is comforting to know that we cannot escape from Your presence, it is sobering to realize that we can hide no sin from You. **You know, O Lord, that we have not strongly resisted sin, nor have we always avoided the circumstances that might lead us into sin.** We have resented Your discipline rather than rejoice that You count us worthy to suffer. **We have often sacrificed Christian principles for the sake of a temporary peace.** We have remained silent when we should have given testimony in Your defense. **We have compromised with evil rather than take a stand for You.** For these and countless other offenses, forgive us, O Lord.

To consistently live to Your honor and glory, we need Your help, O Lord. Send us Your Holy Spirit that He may lift our drooping hands and strengthen our weak knees. **Guide our spiritual feet on the straight path that leads to You, and help us follow in the footsteps of our Savior.** May Your abiding presence bring peace to the troubled soul, companionship to the lonely, hope to the discouraged, and healing to the sick.

(*Here special intercessions, silent or spoken, may be made. If spoken, each portion concludes:* Lord, in Your mercy, **hear our prayer.**)

Accept our thanks for hearing our prayers. **We offer them in the name of our Lord and Savior Jesus Christ. Amen**

FOURTEENTH SUNDAY AFTER PENTECOST

Almighty and everlasting Father, we bring You our praise and adoration. **For the beautiful world, which You created to be our habitat, we give You thanks.** For the breath of life, which You nourish within us, we are deeply grateful. **For our reason and senses, which enable us to enjoy Your creation, we give You thanks.** For the gift of salvation, assured to us through the redemption of Your Son Jesus Christ, we praise Your most holy name.

We confess that we are unworthy of Your gifts of mercy. Through the concern and love of others who have shared the Gospel with us, Your Holy Spirit has brought us into Your kingdom. **For not being sufficiently concerned about those who do not know that they too can have salvation, forgive us, O Lord.** Having enjoyed the privilege of being in Your kingdom, we often become overconfident that we can never fall away from Your grace. **For our neglect of Your Word and sacraments, forgive us, O Lord.** For our neglect in performing our daily tasks to Your honor and glory, forgive us, O Lord. **For our lack of zeal to labor in Your kingdom, we ask Your forgiveness.**

May Your Holy Spirit keep us in Your kingdom through faith in our Lord and Savior Jesus Christ. **Strengthen us so that we can perform our daily tasks to Your honor and glory.** Kindle in our hearts that divine love which enables us to rejoice in serving You and others. **Use us to alleviate the suffering of the poor, to provide fellowship for the lonely, and to be a source of hope to the discouraged.**

(*Here special intercessions, silent or spoken, may be made. If spoken, each portion concludes:* Lord, in Your mercy, **hear our prayer.**)

In the name of our compassionate Savior, **we pray. Amen**

FIFTEENTH SUNDAY AFTER PENTECOST

Lord God, heavenly Father, we gratefully acknowledge Your kind providence, which has sheltered us until this hour. **As we consider Your manifold kindnesses to us, we humbly thank You for Your gracious presence.** Accept our praises for Your creation, our redemption, and our sanctification. **We fear no evil because our hearts firmly trust in You.**

Certainly we have no reason to be proud of ourselves. **Without You we are nothing; without You we could do nothing.** You have called us saints through Christ Jesus, our Lord, and yet we are still sinners. **We are too ready to exalt ourselves over others, seeking places of honor.** We are too ready to repay evil for evil. **We have cursed when we should have blessed.** We have been sowers of discord instead of being instruments of Your peace. **We have failed to overcome evil with good.** For these our many transgressions, forgive us, O Lord.

Send us Your Holy Spirit that we may grow in the grace and knowledge of Jesus Christ, our Lord. Give us the right words to say when our neighbor rejoices and when our neighbor weeps. **Give us a true spirit of humility that rejoices in another's good fortune.** Give us a generous heart that we may share our bounty with the needy. **Help us to comfort the bereaved and minister to the sick.** Help us to forgive as we have been forgiven.

(*Here special intercessions, silent or spoken, may be made. If spoken, each portion concludes:* Lord, in Your mercy, **hear our prayer.**)

We ask this in the name of Him, who humbled Himself unto death, **even the death of the cross, Jesus Christ, our Lord. Amen**

SIXTEENTH SUNDAY AFTER PENTECOST

Dear heavenly Father, we, Your children in Christ, come before You with our praises. **For the breath of life and for the fresh air, which sustains our life, we give You thanks.** For the food that nourishes our bodies and for the spiritual food that nurtures our souls, we give You thanks. **But especially, O Lord, we thank You for our redemption in Christ Jesus.**

We acknowledge, O Lord, that as Your children, we fall woefully short of the requirements for discipleship. **Time and again we have permitted our concerns for family and friends to interfere with our commitments to You and Your Son.** We have often claimed too glibly to be Christians, without seriously considering the cost. **Instead of being wholehearted in maximum service, we have too often been halfhearted in minimal service.** We readily admit that we have been guilty of loving the world too much and loving You too little. **We have not borne our own crosses willingly, and we have not renounced everything to follow You.** For these and all our transgressions, forgive us, O Lord.

Revive our faith, O Lord, with Your Holy Spirit. Give us quiet minds and hearts to accept the things we cannot change.

Give us courage to change the things that interfere with our discipleship. Give us wisdom to make choices in accordance with Your will.

Extend Your healing hand to the sick, Your peace to the troubled, and Your strength to the weak.

(*Here special intercessions, silent or spoken, may be made. If spoken, each portion concludes:* Lord, in Your mercy, **hear our prayer.**)

Grant peace to our nation, and help us to live in harmony with Your will. **We pray in Jesus' name. Amen**

SEVENTEENTH SUNDAY AFTER PENTECOST

God of mercy and God of truth, we come before You in worship and praise. **For sending us Your Son to lead us through the wilderness of this world's sin into the promised land of Your forgiveness, we give You thanks.** For having found us among the millions of straying and lost sheep, we give You thanks. **You have proven Yourself to be mighty in deed and plenteous in mercy, for which we praise and adore You.**

And yet, O Lord, in spite of Your loving-kindness toward us, we confess that we have often sinned against You. **Again and again You have demonstrated Your almighty power by leading us through many troubled waters, but we have sought human resources rather than coming to You.** For our many sins of disloyalty and failure to acknowledge Your leadership among us, forgive us, O Lord. **For doubting Your promises and trusting in our own merits, forgive us, O Lord.**

Send us Your Holy Spirit that He may guide us into all truth. **As You have had patience with us, so may we have patience with others.** As You have found us lost sinners and brought us back to Your fold, so may we diligently seek the lost and bring them to the knowledge of salvation through Christ. **As heaven rejoices over one sinner who repents, give us the joy of leading someone to Christ.**

(*Here special intercessions, silent or spoken, may be made. If spoken, each portion concludes:* Lord, in Your mercy, **hear our prayer.**)

May Your mercy, O Lord, be a source of strength to the weak, healing power to the sick, and hope to the discouraged. **To You, the only true God, through Jesus Christ be honor and glory forever and ever. Amen**

EIGHTEENTH SUNDAY AFTER PENTECOST

With praise and adoration we come before You, O Lord God of mercy. **By Your grace we greet the morning light of a new day, and by Your grace we shall be alive to praise You in the evening.** We are grateful to You for our physical preservation but especially adore You for sending Your Son as the only Mediator between ourselves and Your divine majesty.

In spite of Your goodness we confess that we have sinned against and offended Your holiness. We have not been able to walk before You perfectly. **We have failed to pray diligently for all who are in authority.** We have not always practiced good stewardship of that which You have entrusted to our care. **We have often brought discredit to Your name by not paying our bills as promptly as possible.** We have often overlooked the importance of being faithful in small matters while seeking important positions in Your kingdom. **We have been guilty of halfhearted service for You while trying to please the secular world.** For these and all our transgressions, we beg Your forgiveness.

Assured of forgiveness through our Lord Jesus Christ, we are bold to ask You to grant our petitions. Endow the leaders of our nation with integrity and honor. **Grant that the heads of all nations consider their power as a trust from You, and grant that they administer that power for the benefit of all.** Help us exercise good stewardship for the upbuilding of Your kingdom and the welfare of all people.

(*Here special intercessions, silent or spoken, may be made. If spoken, each portion concludes:* Lord, in Your mercy, **hear our prayer.**)

In faith that You will hear our prayer, **we pray in the name of our Lord Jesus Christ. Amen**

NINETEENTH SUNDAY AFTER PENTECOST

We praise You, O Lord; we will praise You as long as we live. **Our trust in people has so often been fruitless, but You, O Lord, can be trusted from generation to generation.** You have lifted us from the valley of despair to the mountain of hope through Your Son Jesus Christ. **Through Him we are assured that salvation is ours; He has given our earthly lives meaning and purpose.**

And yet, O Lord, we do not always reflect the joy of the hope in our lives. **We are so easily drawn to the things of this earth.** In the pursuit of our own interests we often forget the poor at our door and in the world. **We spend millions on beverages when there are millions who need a drink of water.** We complain about the high cost of food and forget that there are many who cannot buy food at any price because there is none. **We are served in countless ways by our technology while millions must scrounge for a living.** Not only are we guilty of being stingy with our material wealth, but we are also reluctant to share the treasure of the Gospel with others. **For our self-centeredness and lack of concern for the physically and spiritually poor, we implore Your forgiveness.**

Give us a spirit of compassion and generosity. **Help us follow Your Word, given to us by Moses and the prophets and by Your living Word, Jesus Christ.**

(*Here special intercessions, silent or spoken, may be made. If spoken, each portion concludes:* Lord, in Your mercy, **hear our prayer.**)

Bless our nation with peace, and help us dwell in harmony with Your will. **In the name of Him who died that we might live, even Jesus Christ, our Lord. Amen**

TWENTIETH SUNDAY AFTER PENTECOST

O Lord God, King of kings, our hearts are filled with songs of joy as we acknowledge that You are the Rock of our salvation. **We come into Your presence with thanksgiving and into Your courts with praise.** We praise You for making us the people of Your pasture and the sheep of Your hand by sending us Your Son Jesus Christ.

You have given us every reason to rejoice, and we have given You every reason to be sad. It is so much easier to praise You with our words than to praise You with our lives. **When our lives nullify the words of praise that come from our lips, forgive us, O Lord.** You have made us righteous through Christ, but we have so often failed to live by our faith. **We have been neglectful in witnessing to our Lord, and we have hesitated to share in suffering for the Gospel.** Not only have we surrendered to the temptation to sin, but we have also been guilty of leading others into sin. **We have lacked the courage to correct our brothers and sisters, and we have been reluctant to forgive.** For these and other transgressions of which we may not be aware, forgive us, O Lord.

Send us Your Holy Spirit that He may lead us into all truth. Strengthen our faith to believe that Your almighty power can remove the mountains of our cares and anxieties. **May Your presence be felt in the halls of our congress and in the councils of nations.** May Your name be glorified and Your laws obeyed.

(*Here special intercessions, silent or spoken, may be made. If spoken, each portion concludes:* Lord, in Your mercy, **hear our prayer.**)

Alleviate the suffering of the sick, assure the lonely of Your presence, and give hope to the discouraged. **In the name of Jesus our Savior, we pray. Amen**

TWENTY-FIRST SUNDAY AFTER PENTECOST

Lord God, heavenly Father, we come before You with thanksgiving. **We praise You for Your mighty works which exceed anything we can think or do.** With a mighty hand You delivered Your chosen people from the shackles of slavery. **With an even mightier hand You raised Your Son Jesus Christ from the dead.** Through Him we, who trust in Him as our Savior, have the hope of eternal life. **For this, the mightiest of all works, we give You humble and hearty thanks.**

As we thank and praise You, O Lord, we realize how thankless and ungrateful we have often been in the past. **We have been like the nine lepers who went on their way, enjoying Your merciful gifts but forgetting to give You thanks.** The leprosy of sin still clings to us, O Lord, and prevents us from giving You the perfect praise due Your most holy name. **Imperfect though it be, accept our thanks for delivering us from the eternal consequences of this leprosy.** In the name of Jesus Christ we beg Your forgiveness; in Your mercy, make us whole.

Send us Your Holy Spirit that He may strengthen our faith and help us to accept Your forgiveness through Jesus Christ, our Lord. May our lives constantly reflect our gratitude for Your great mercy. **Give us the courage to witness to our faith in Christ that others may obtain life in His name.**

(Here special intercessions, silent or spoken, may be made. If spoken, each portion concludes: Lord in Your mercy, **hear our prayer.**)

May Your mighty power, as revealed in Your Word, be a source of healing power to the sick. **Accept our praise and thanksgiving in the name of Jesus Christ, our Lord. Amen**

TWENTY-SECOND SUNDAY AFTER PENTECOST

We lift our eyes to You, O Lord, who made heaven and earth. **You have kept watch while we slept.** You have kept us from all evil; You have preserved our souls. **In the midst of trouble You have been our source of unfailing help.** You have delivered us from the burden of our sins through our Lord Jesus Christ. **For Your innumerable mercies we give You humble and hearty thanks.**

We confess, O Lord, that in spite of Your many mercies, we have displeased You with our sins. **Although You have assured us that every word in Your Scriptures was inspired by the Holy Spirit, we cannot fully understand it.** We get disturbed when we cannot fathom the depth and height of Your infinite truth. **We confess that in attempting to solve our problems we have often resorted to human reason rather than search Your Word for the answer.** In our desire to be modern we have had itching ears for new doctrines. **Although You have urged us to pray always and not lose heart, we have been lazy in praying.** We have failed to wrestle with You until You blessed us. **For these and countless other sins, forgive us, O Lord.**

May Your Holy Spirit guide our finite minds into Your infinite truth. **Help us to be faithful to sound doctrine as we have been taught.** Give us diligence in prayer and faith to believe that Your blessings will come.

Be with our nation's president, the congress of the United States, and the governors of our commonwealths. Bless our nation with peace, and help us to live in harmony with Your will.

(*Here special intercessions, silent or spoken, may be made. If spoken, each portion concludes:* Lord, in Your mercy, **hear our prayer.**)

This we ask in the name of Jesus Christ, our Lord, **who lives and reigns with You and the Holy Spirit, one God forever. Amen**

TWENTY-THIRD SUNDAY AFTER PENTECOST

We praise You, O Lord; we exalt Your most holy name. **In the midst of trouble we praise You for Your goodness.** Though our lot on earth may not always be easy and pleasant, Your mercies have been our strength and stay. **To know that You have chosen us to be Your own is all we need to know to make life worth living.**

We confess that we are not worthy of all Your blessings. **We have exalted ourselves when we should have been humble.** We have thought highly of ourselves while despising others. **We have not always served You nor walked in Your ways.** We have not loved You with all of our hearts, souls, and minds. **We have weakened in the good fight of faith.** We have been discouraged, forgetting that Your power is ours for the asking. **We have overlooked many opportunities to spread Your Gospel.** We have been proud of our goodness when we should have proclaimed Your justice and mercy. **For these, our many sins, we beg Your forgiveness.**

May Your Holy Spirit strengthen our faith. **Give us a spirit of true humility to recognize the merits of others.** Help us to be concerned about the spiritual and physical wellbeing of all who dwell on the face of the earth. **Bless the witness of our words and lives on the hearts of those who do not know You.**

(*Here special intercessions, silent or spoken, may be made. If spoken, each portion concludes:* Lord, in Your mercy, **hear our prayer.**)

When we have finished the race, grant us the crown of righteousness earned by our Lord and Savior Jesus Christ. **We pray in His name. Amen**

TWENTY-FOURTH SUNDAY AFTER PENTECOST

We extol You, our God, and will bless Your name forever. **You are gracious and full of compassion, slow to anger, and of great mercy.** You are good to all, and Your tender mercies are over all Your works. **You open Your hand and satisfy the desires of every living thing.** You are near to all who call upon You, who call upon You in truth. **You have heard our cries and saved us through Jesus Christ, our Lord.**

As we have found favor in Your sight through Christ, may Your divine presence be in our midst, pardon our iniquity, and take us for Your inheritance. **Grant us a rich measure of Your grace, and send us peace through our Lord Jesus Christ.** May our faith grow abundantly and our love for one another increase. **May we fulfill every good resolve and work through Your power.** May the name of our Lord Jesus Christ be glorified in us according to Your grace.

As our Lord's association with Zacchaeus changed his life, so may the Savior's association with us change our lives. May our faith in Him cause us to give to the poor and keep us from defrauding our neighbor.

May Your Holy Spirit increase our faith. Exert Your power for peace among the nations of the earth. **Endow those in authority in our land to rule in justice and mercy.** May the lonely experience Your presence and the sorrowing Your comfort. **Grant Your healing to the sick and Your courage to the disheartened.**

(*Here special intercessions, silent or spoken, may be made. If spoken, each portion concludes:* Lord, in Your mercy, **hear our prayer.**)

Accept our praise and thanks for all Your mercies. **This we ask in the name of Jesus Christ, our Lord and Savior. Amen**

TWENTY-FIFTH SUNDAY AFTER PENTECOST

Lord God, heavenly Father, with all creation we lift up our voices to You in praise for Your loving-kindness. **Yours is the greatness, power, glory, victory, and majesty.** Both riches and honor come from You according to Your grace through our Lord Jesus Christ. **In Your hand are power and might, and by Your hand You make great and give strength to all.** We thank You, our God, and praise Your glorious name.

We confess that in spite of Your power and loving-kindness we have often permitted fear to enter our hearts. When we consider the multitude of sins we have committed, we often doubt Your grace to cover them all. **As we observe the ungodly and the evil they do, we often forget that Your Word is powerful enough to triumph over every evil deed and word.** We have not always left judgment in Your hands but have felt that we must execute retribution. **For these and all our transgressions, forgive us, O Lord, for Your Son's sake.**

Send us Your Holy Spirit that He may comfort our hearts with faith in Your continuing love and mercy. **Set our minds and hearts on Your promises of eternal life through Your Son Jesus Christ.** May Your assurance of our resurrection give us hope to survive an evil day. **Hasten the day of Your coming when we can enjoy the company of Abraham, Isaac, and Jacob and all the saints whom You have already called to Yourself.**

(*Here special intercessions, silent or spoken, may be made. If spoken, each portion concludes:* Lord, in Your mercy, **hear our prayer.**)

May the hope of our resurrection strengthen us to live our lives to Your honor and glory. **Hear our prayer in the name of Him who is the Resurrection and the Life. Amen**

THIRD-LAST SUNDAY IN THE CHURCH YEAR

We sing a new song to You, O Lord, for You have done marvelous things. **Your right hand and Your holy arm have brought You victory.** Your victory over Satan, death, and the grave has spread Your name to the ends of the earth. **All nature joins in to sing Your praises.** Musical instruments join in the chorus of rejoicing when You come to the earth to judge it with righteousness and equity.

We confess, O Lord, that we deserve Your righteous indignation and displeasure. As Israel stirred up Your anger by worshiping the golden calf, so our generation likewise has incurred Your displeasure. **Gold is still one of the idols of our world, and we have often worshiped it.** We too are guilty of idolatry when we love and trust in our money and possessions more than we do in You. **For often making the love of money the center of our lives, forgive us, O Lord.**

Help us not to ignore Your warnings of the coming of the last day. **As we enjoy the abundance of Your gifts, grant that they do not lead us into carelessness and irresponsibility.** May Your kingdom dwell among us as we enjoy each other's fellowship here on earth.

Grant Your blessings to our efforts to speed on the coming of Your kingdom. Strengthen us and guard us from evil. **Keep us in Your love and in steadfastness to Jesus Christ, our Lord and Savior.**

May the lonely experience Your presence, the sorrowing Your comfort, the sick Your healing, and the disheartened Your courage.

(*Here special intercessions, silent or spoken, may be made. If spoken, each portion concludes:* Lord, in Your mercy, **hear our prayer.**)

Bless the leaders of our nation, state, and church with wisdom and insight. **Grant harmony among the nations of the world. This we ask in Jesus' name. Amen**

THIRD-LAST SUNDAY IN THE CHURCH YEAR (Alternate)

We sing Your praises, O Lord, for You have done marvelous things. **Your judgments in the past have always been right and just.** Therefore, in the Final Judgment You will make all things right. **The wicked, who have caused us much concern, will get their just rewards.** There has been much injustice in the world; therefore, it is comforting for us to know that You will judge with equity. **For those who fear Your name, the sun of righteousness shall rise with healing in its wings.**

We confess that we have not always lived as if time were of the essence. **We have squandered a goodly portion of our lives by being overly concerned with vain and useless things.** Even though we may not be gainfully employed, we have no excuse for idleness. **For our indolence and lethargy, forgive us, O Lord.**

Send us Your Holy Spirit that He may help us to be more productive workers. **When the world condemns us for our faith, help us to testify to the truth.** When the world persecutes us for believing in Your Son Jesus Christ, help us not to be dismayed. **Give us the courage and the words we need to refute Your enemies.** Help us not to be led astray by false teachers.

(*Here special intercessions, silent or spoken, may be made. If spoken, each portion concludes:* Lord, in Your mercy, **hear our prayer.**)

Bless our nation with peace, and help us dwell in harmony with Your will. **Help Your Church accomplish its primary mission, and assure us of Your presence. In Jesus' name we pray. Amen**

SECOND-LAST SUNDAY IN THE CHURCH YEAR

It is good for us to give thanks to You, O Lord, and to sing praises to Your name, O Most High. **We declare Your steadfast love in the morning and Your faithfulness by night.** You have made us glad to do Your work; at the work of Your hands we sing for joy. **Your works are very great, O Lord, and Your thoughts are very deep.** Your merciful kindness to the wicked is beyond our understanding.

We confess, O Lord, that we have often fallen away from You. We have turned our backs on our responsibilities to Your kingdom. **We have often acted stubbornly, failing to acknowledge the error of our ways.** You have entrusted us all with at least one talent. **We have not always used these talents in Your service.** For phantasizing about how wonderful it will be when we no longer need to face the problems of living in this world, instead of getting to work, **forgive us, O Lord.**

Send us Your Holy Spirit that He may lift us up when we fall, turn us back when we have turned away, and give us hope and courage to face reality. **May it be our sole desire to please You and Jesus Christ, whom You have sent.**

Remember in Your mercy those who are suffering through no fault of their own. **Be with the refugees of war-torn countries.** Alleviate the sufferings of those who have been victims of crime, and bring criminals to justice.

(*Here special intercessions, silent or spoken, may be made. If spoken, each portion concludes:* Lord in Your mercy, **hear our prayer.**)

Bless our nation with peace, and terminate conflict throughout the world. **Hear our prayer for Jesus' sake. Amen**

LAST SUNDAY IN THE CHURCH YEAR
Sunday of the Fulfillment

Out of the depths we cry to You, O Lord, Lord hear our voice. **We wait for You, O Lord, our souls wait, and in Your Word we hope.** As anxious as the night watchman is to see the sun rise, so we eagerly watch for the coming of the Son of Righteousness. **We hope in You, O Lord, for with You is steadfast love and plenteous redemption.**

We confess that we are often disturbed by the seeming good fortune of the wicked. **They so often seem to prosper more than the righteous and yet go unpunished for their crimes.** Your prophets promise that there will be a day of divine reckoning when a distinction will be made between those who serve You and those who do not. **Help us not to seek revenge, but instill in our hearts a love that will not let them go.** Give us courage to confront the wicked with the knowledge of Your way. **Send Your Holy Spirit that He may add power to the words of our testimony.**

Help us, O Lord, to honor our responsiblities as good stewards of Your possessions. **Keep us from overexerting our authority, and help us to treat all people with respect and love.** According to Your will grant that we also be treated with respect and love. **Help us not to sin in ignorance, and help us to make allowances for those who do.** Grant good health to all, especially to those who are of the household of faith. **Pardon the penitent, be a companion to the lonely, and give hope to the discouraged.**

(*Here special intercessions, silent or spoken, may be made. If spoken, each portion concludes:* Lord, in Your mercy, **hear our prayer.**)

Look favorably upon our land, and bless Your people with peace. **Grant these our requests in the name of Jesus, our Savior. Amen**

LAST SUNDAY IN THE CHURCH YEAR
Sunday of the Fulfillment (Alternate)

Lord God, heavenly Father, we come before You with hearts that are grateful for giving us a Savior who rose triumphant over the grave. **When it seemed He had been overcome by the forces of evil at the hands of sinful men, You raised Him from the dead.** You have now exalted Him above every power in heaven and earth, where He reigns as King of kings and Lord of lords.

Send us Your Holy Spirit that Christ may also rule in our hearts. As the world longs for peace and tries to establish it by force of arms and political power, help us to realize that each of us, as subjects of our King, has the responsibility to live peaceably with our neighbor. **Help us conquer the forces of hate with Your love and the forces of injustice with Your justice.** Help us thwart the devastating power of hunger with Your abundance and the devitalizing power of sickness with Your healing.

O Lord Jesus Christ, Head of the Church, we ask You to use us to heal the wounds of schism in the Church. Give us the spirit of wisdom and understanding. **Help us to understand with patience those who in sincere loyalty to You are sometimes misunderstood even by their fellow Christians.** Give us open minds and hearts to listen with love. **Help us to refrain from judging and misjudging our brothers and sisters in the faith.** May Your Church present to the world a harmonious and united front.

(*Here special intercessions, silent or spoken, may be made. If spoken, each portion concludes:* Lord, in Your mercy, **hear our prayer.**)

Add Your blessing to our witness that You are King of kings and Lord of lords. **In Jesus' name we pray. Amen**

PRAYERS FOR MINOR FESTIVALS AND OCCASIONS

Series A, B, C

NEW YEAR'S DAY

O merciful heavenly Father, by Your grace we enter another new year. **We praise and glorify Your holy name.** By Your creative power You have sustained our lives and protected us through many dangers. **For Your abundant blessings we give You most hearty thanks.**

Assured of the forgiveness of our sins through the name of Your Son Jesus, we take another step into the future. **Although we do not know what lies ahead, we proceed with confidence, trusting You to be with us.** Whether the year ahead brings sickness or health, poverty or riches, sadness or joy, **we know that You will give us guidance and strength.**

In accordance with Your will that at the name of Jesus every knee should bow, **use us to tell the world that You have highly exalted Him above every other name.** To this end bless the witness of Your Church on earth. **May the members of our congregation and church body proclaim His name through all the world.** Grant unity, peace, and love to Your people that their witness might be accepted with open hearts.

(*Here special intercessions, silent or spoken, may be made. If spoken, each portion concludes:* Lord, in Your mercy, **hear our prayer.**)

O Lord, grant peace among the nations in the year ahead. **Grant that we may proceed in harmony with the mission You have placed before us.** Assure us that You are with us in all our trials, setbacks, and victories. **This we ask in the name of Your Son Jesus. Amen**

REFORMATION DAY

Since the beginning of time, O Lord, You have spoken to humanity. **Even though people have sought to silence Your voice, You have pierced the vale of silence with Your powerful Word.** Through Moses and the prophets You made Your will known among us. **When Your messages were ignored, You miraculously embodied Your Word in the person of Jesus Christ.** Again some tried to still Your voice by nailing Your Word to a cross, **but You could not be silenced.** You raised Your "Word made flesh" from the dead so that many have heard the message. **We thank You, Lord, that we have heard the message through Christ.**

Many have been the heroes and saints who have, at great personal sacrifice, handed the Gospel on to us today. **Many sacrificed their lives in the defense of Your truth and the Gospel.** In spite of their efforts, however, human barriers have often curtailed the free distribution, teaching, and preaching of Your Word. **Many times Your Word has been buried under the rubble of man-made laws and traditions.** But You have always brought forth one of Your chosen servants to restore Your Word. **For giving us such men to lead us out of spiritual darkness into the marvelous light of the Gospel, we give You thanks.**

Help us, O Lord, to treasure Your Word, and guard it with a due sense of appreciation for those who have made its presence in our midst possible. **Help us to read, hear, and inwardly digest it so that we may grow in the knowledge of our Lord Jesus Christ, in whose name we pray. Amen**

DAY OF NATIONAL THANKSGIVING

Most gracious God, who gives us so freely of Your bounty, **we call to remembrance in glad thanksgiving Your lovingkindness and tender mercies.** For the world in which we live, for its fruitfulness and order, for its beauty and its wonder, and for the life You have given us here to enjoy, we praise You, O God. **For our home, for our families and friends, for the fellowship we share, and for the love that lifts our hearts and nurtures our spirits, we praise You, O God.** For the common blessings of our everyday life, for food and clothing, for shelter and rest, for work and leisure, we praise You, O Lord. **For this land we love, for our nation's heritage of liberty, for the sacrifices of our forefathers, for all noble hopes and efforts that mankind may be one in brotherhood and peace, we thank You, Lord.** For Your gracious gifts to our minds and spirits, for memory that links us to the past, for hope that leads us to the future, for courage in times of trouble, for patience in tribulation, for wisdom in perplexity, for faith in every moment and love at all times, we thank You, heavenly Father. **For Yourself, O God, for Your majesty and power, for Your wisdom and goodness, for Your justice and truth, for Your Son, Your blessed Gift of love through whom we have the forgiveness of all our sins, for Your Holy Spirit, enlightening our hearts, we thank You, O God.**

(*Here special thanksgivings, silent or spoken, may be made. If spoken, each portion concludes:* Lord, in Your mercy, **hear our prayer.**)

So direct us in thought, word, and deed that our gratitude may be reflected in how we live. **In the name of Jesus Christ, our Savior. Amen**